The Biracial *and* Multiracial Student Experience

To my granddaughter, Eva Salomé Àlvarez Davis
Born December 30, 2007
You are the future!

The Biracial and Multiracial Student Experience

A Journey to Racial Literacy

Bonnie M.
DAVIS

CORWIN
A SAGE Company

For information:

Corwin
A SAGE Company
2455 Teller Road
Thousand Oaks, California 91320
(800) 233-9936
Fax: (800) 417-2466
www.corwinpress.com

SAGE Ltd.
1 Oliver's Yard
55 City Road
London EC1Y 1SP
United Kingdom

SAGE India Pvt. Ltd.
B 1/I 1 Mohan Cooperative
    Industrial Area
Mathura Road, New Delhi 110 044
India

SAGE Asia-Pacific Pte. Ltd.
33 Pekin Street #02-01
Far East Square
Singapore 048763

Printed in the United States of America.

Library of Congress Cataloging-in-Publication Data

Davis, Bonnie M.
The biracial and multiracial student experience : A journey to racial literacy / Bonnie M. Davis.
    p. cm.
Includes bibliographical references and index.
ISBN 978-1-4129-7505-6 (cloth)
ISBN 978-1-4129-7506-3 (pbk.)

1. Racially mixed people—Education—United States. 2. Multicultural education—United States. 3. Teacher-student relationships—United States. I. Title.

LC3621.D39 2009
371.829'0500973—dc22   2009010946

This book is printed on acid-free paper.

09   10   11   12   13   10   9   8   7   6   5   4   3   2   1

Acquisitions Editor:	Dan Alpert
Associate Editor:	Megan Bedell
Production Editor:	Eric Garner
Copy Editor:	Jeannette McCoy
Typesetter:	C&M Digitals (P) Ltd.
Proofreader:	Susan Schon
Indexer:	Sheila Bodell
Cover Designer:	Rose Storey

Contents

Acknowledgments

The more books I write, the more I learn how much I depend on others. First, thank you, Dan Alpert, my editor at Corwin. Dan is so exceptional: he knows when you need a phone call; he understands your feelings; and he gives you the feedback you need to succeed. Along with Dan, Mary Kim Schreck, friend and fellow author, offered me feedback and solace as she was writing her own book.

Thanks to Kim Anderson. Kim first suggested I write a book in 2000, and then she did everything to make it happen. She formatted my writing, bound and printed it, and set up a Web site to promote it. For this book, too, she was there every step of the way.

A big thanks goes out to Ruth Dambach, my sister, who has been by my side throughout the process of each of my books. She reads my writing, edits, formats, and ensures it all gets done. She is always there for me as are the rest of my family—my sisters, Susan and Mary, and my dad.

Thanks to my dear friends who supported me during this process: Elizabeth Krekeler, Nan Starling, Julie Heifetz, Tina Lombardo, and Nancy Saguto. They patiently listened to me and offered advice when asked. Hugs to Dorothy Kelly, who contributed to my first book and continues to help me learn *what I don't know I don't know.*

Thanks to Glenn Singleton and Curtis Linton for their groundbreaking work in the area of *Courageous Conversations About Race.* I have learned so much from them. Thanks also to the reviewers who read the draft and responded with comments that caused me to extensively revise the book. A special thanks to Randy Lindsey who took the time to meet with me and offer his sage advice.

I have to acknowledge the team I have worked with in St. Louis since 1997 at Cooperating School Districts. Dennis Lubeck, Sheila Onuska, Sue Heggarty, Mike Grady, and Megan Moncure have provided a professional family for me through all the changes that have occurred in the last decade. Thank you!

A very special thanks goes to all the individuals who contributed their narratives for the book and to those individuals, such as Charles Rankin,

Jon Clark, Gloria Barajas, Jane Bannester, and Sarah Riss, who solicited students for me to interview. The book would *not* exist without the support of all of these individuals. These individuals shared personal and often-times private experiences so we could better learn about the lives of mixed-identity children and their families. You can find their names listed below. I am especially grateful to my son, Reeve, and his partner, Brenda, and to my daughter, Leah, for sharing their stories for mom's book. Thank you. Last, but never least, thanks to Fred, my dancing partner in life.

Thanks also to the Corwin team: Acquisitions Editor Dan Alpert, Associate Editor Megan Bedell, Production Editor Eric Garner, Copy Editor Jeannette McCoy, Typesetter C&M Digitals (P) Ltd., Proofreader Susan Schon, Indexer Sheila Bodell, and Cover Designer Rose Storey.

The individuals listed below contributed narratives to the book:

Brenda Àlvarez

Leah Ancona

Kim Anderson

Christina Amalia Andrade

Francesca Maria Apodaca

Mani Barajas-Alexander

Donna Beard

Edith Beard Brady

Chelsea Breckenridge

Diana Breckenridge

Glynnis Breckenridge

Stan Breckenridge

Alicia Cooper (pseudonym)

Kay Cornell

Courtnee Cox

Taylor Donaven Crask

Reeve Davis

Jennifer Duncan

Alicia Edison

Jacqueline Felgate

April Warren Grice

Karen Hayes

Maria Hernandez

Rufina Hernandez

Alex Hudgens

Bassam Khawaja

Kim Kouri

Chris Lent

Curtis Linton

Dennis Lubeck

Tahnee Markussen

Ashley Meyer

Graig Meyer

Alicia Notarainni

Karen Notarainni

Wil Parker

Charlane Pralle-Janssen

Joseph Rousseau

Val Shumate

Michael Tapp

Michael Vaughn

About the Author

 **Bonnie M. Davis**, PhD, is the author of the best-selling Corwin book *How to Teach Students Who Don't Look Like You: Culturally Relevant Teaching Strategies* (2006) and *How to Coach Teachers Who Don't Think Like You: Using Literacy Strategies to Coach Across Content Areas* (2007). She currently serves as a consultant on literacy coaching, writing across the content areas, and culturally proficient instruction to schools, districts, and professional organizations.

For 30 years, she taught English in middle schools, high schools, universities, homeless shelters, and a men's prison. She is the recipient of several awards, including The Teacher of the Year, the Governor's Award for Teaching Excellence, and the Anti-Defamation League's World of Difference Community Service Award. She holds a PhD in English from Saint Louis University.

Her publications include *African-American Academic Achievement: Building a Classroom of Excellence* (2001) and numerous articles on literacy and cultural instruction, such as "A Cultural Safari," a National Council of Teachers of English (NCTE) Paul Farmer Writing Award runner-up winner, and the cover article in the Missouri National Education Association's (MNEA) publication, *Something Better* (Winter, 2006). She appears in the School Improvement Network's video program, *No Excuses! How to Increase Minority Student Achievement* (2006), and is coauthor along with Curtis Linton of a guidebook for the series.

In addition to her writing, Bonnie spends her professional life coaching and presenting to educators. She has presented at National Staff Development Council (NSDC), National Council of Teachers of English (NCTE), Association for Supervision and Curriculum Development (ASCD), International Reading Association (IRA), National Association for Multicultural Education (NAME), and various other national and state conferences. Because she spent 30 years in the classroom, she considers herself first a teacher, and she relates to staffs in a lively, interactive manner.

When she works with educators, Bonnie is passionate, funny, and energetic, modeling for staff instructional and relationship strategies to improve achievement and foster equity for all students.

A former Midwesterner, she currently lives in Southern California and is available for keynotes, presentations, workshops, and consultation. You can reach her at a4achievement@earthlink.net or view her Web site at www.educatingforchange.com.

Prologue

Dear Reader,

Welcome to a journey of self-discovery. Since you chose to read this book, you must be interested in learning about the impact of race upon your students, and in particular, children identified as biracial or multiracial students. This book is an endeavor to examine what educators need to know about multiracial students presented in the format of a learning journey.

As with any journey, we begin in one place and end in another. The place where we end may not be, and probably will not be, the destination we had planned, but that is part of what makes it exciting. For this journey, we need our minds and our hearts as we embark on a journey to cultural proficiency. Cultural proficiency is a "mindset for how we interact with all people, irrespective of their cultural memberships" (Terrell & Lindsey, 2009, p. 21). It is a worldview, and the lens through which we see the world. It is "who we are, more than what we do" (p. 20). Our journey is about cultural proficiency.

The journey to cultural proficiency includes creating spaces for individuals who differ from us then listening to their stories and learning from them. As we reflect and interact with the racial narratives found in the book, we develop racial literacy. Racial literacy is the ability to "talk with people in order to understand and address racially loaded controversies" (Bolgatz, J. p. 1). I would add it is the ability to be fluent about issues of race and to understand the power and impact it has upon us and the students in our classrooms.

In order to be fluent about issues of race and address racially loaded controversies, we must engage in courageous conversations about race. To do this, we need a guide. I found a guide in Glenn Singleton and Curtis Linton's book *Courageous Conversations About Race: A Field Guide for Achieving Equity in Schools* (2006). The book provides a framework for dialogue about race and informs the journey I take with this book.

I recently read an article that spoke to the differences between young people (born after 1980) and those of earlier generations. The new generation values transparency and disclosure; earlier generations tended to believe more in "minding one's own business" and "keeping it in the family." Transparency and disclosure is everywhere in our present society. Reality shows speak to this phenomenon as do Web sites, such as Facebook, text messaging, Wikipedia, and all the other technology sites and tools that allow us to know where our friends are and what they are doing any minute of the day. We live much more public lives, should we decide to do so.

This book mirrors that new transparency and disclosure. The people in this book volunteered to disclose their private lives so we could better understand the cultural lens of those who live lives of mixed identity. This is their reality. Each of us struggles to understand reality and what we can do to better navigate our reality. My hope is that this book offers a vehicle to navigate your reality in a fresh new way in hopes we can grow together to better understand what we *don't know we don't know* about others' realities. Why do we do this? To give meaning to others' lives and to our own. We seek to understand so we can be better at what we do.

HOW DID THE JOURNEY BEGIN FOR ME?

The journey to understand multiracial students began with the birth of my children. As a white mother of multiracial children, I felt the need to learn what I could about the impact of race upon my children, my students, and me. You will learn more of my racial history in this book. Even though this book is written from the cultural perspective of a white woman, it is written for anyone who works with the cultural mosaic of students who fill today's schools.

WHAT CAUSED ME TO WRITE THIS BOOK?

Two things happened around the same time. I wanted to write a book for educators on multiracial students and found an editor who believed in the project. I began my research during the year I became a grandmother for the first time. My granddaughter is multiracial. She is Black, Mexican, Puerto Rican, and White.

When we drove to the hospital to pick up the birth certificate and accompanying paperwork, an interesting thing happened. They asked Reeve, my son, his race, and he replied, "African American." Brenda, the baby's mother, replied, "Hispanic." Nowhere in the paperwork for my first grandchild was there a mention of my whiteness. I was proud my son was confident of his identity and designated himself as African American, yet I wondered, "Where is the whiteness of my granddaughter?" or "Where am I?" This caused me to wonder even more about the entire equation of race—its designation, power, influence, and control over our lives and the lives of those we love.

WHAT WE *DON'T KNOW WE DON'T KNOW*

Two things—the research for this book and the birth of my granddaughter—catapulted me to a place where I wanted to know more about what I "didn't know I didn't know" about race, racism, and privilege. As a result of this study and writing this book, I think about race, racism, and privilege in a different light.

When I give workshops, I tell educators that we are going to examine "what we don't know we don't know." The journey we take in this book examines the space of not knowing—what is it that I, the author, do not know I don't know? What is it that you, a white educator, don't know you don't know? What is it that you, a monoracial individual who is not white, don't know you don't know? What is it that you, a multiracial individual, don't know you don't know?

WHY THIS BOOK IS AN IMPORTANT JOURNEY FOR YOU

If you feel the need to *know* and to operate from a place where you "know" the answers, the study of racial issues provides more than a bit of discomfort. Even if you relish ambiguity, the study of race offers dissonance and *unknowing* in large spoonfuls. Yet we must journey there. We must create a space for not knowing in order to begin to learn what we don't know about race, what we don't know about racism, and what we don't know about racial privilege. We must create and then leap into a space of not knowing in order to grow as educators and learn how to provide an inclusive racial climate in which all students can thrive. This book offers that space for a journey to do the following:

- examine your own assumptions, values, and beliefs about yourself and others;
- learn from other educators and students who view the world differently from you and interact with their narratives through written responses; and
- develop cultural proficiency, cultural equity, and racial literacy.

WHAT WE CAN LEARN FROM THE MULTIRACIAL STUDENT EXPERIENCE

What is the point of a book about multiracial students? When we examine multiracial students, we create the space to learn more about ourselves, no matter our color or ethnicity, in relation to all of the students in our classes.

The racial narratives in this book remind us there are individuals who in our society are identified as different from any distinct *racial* group, and they cite experiences about which we may be unaware. Often, these experiences reflect the experiences of other students of color since the experiences are the result of being classified or viewed as nonwhite. When this happens, we have additional opportunities to examine the experiences of all students affected by the U.S. racial classification system, and therefore we learn more about the experiences of students of color. However, since there is a growing body of literature about mixed students as a separate group, we can benefit further from knowing what the experts say as well as what self-identified mixed educators and students have to share. This book offers both.

You have an opportunity to learn more about the experiences of self-identified multiracial students and how to equip yourself with strategies to best meet their needs. This does not mean stereotyping mixed students into one generalized group. It cannot logically be done. The vast differences among students who identify as mixed are as varied as the students who identify as not mixed.

This book offers you the following:

- Definitions, histories, and complexities of race
- Opportunities to assess your own knowledge and comfort levels surrounding issues of race
- The challenges students of mixed-racial identity may face that differ from your other students
- A model of professional development
- Strategies you can implement in your educational setting that support multiracial students and their families

My greatest challenge in writing this book has been to present the information in a way that does not accelerate racism. To avoid this, I talked with experts such as Randy Lindsey and Glenn Singleton. Mr. Singleton asked me to consider this question as I wrote the book: "What accelerates racism when dealing with the topic of *multiraciality*?" I used this question as a guide to my thinking and writing. Additionally, I read and *reread* Rainier Spencer's outstanding book *Challenging Multiracial Identities* in the hopes of better understanding this complex topic. His question, "How do we move away from the fallacy of race while remaining aggressive in the battle against racism?'" was another idea I used to guide my work. This book is what I now know I know.

HOW TO USE THIS BOOK

This book is organized as an inductive, *inside-out* journey. It begins with the self and then travels through history and research, interwoven with personal narratives and educational strategies, to culminate with voices of the future—our young people who see a world of change and hope.

Structured as a journey of discovery, this book offers you the opportunity to share your responses to the material with reflection questions. These reflections and responses are *key* to your participation. By the time you finish the chapters and respond to the reflection questions, you will know more about multiracial students in addition to understanding better how race impacts their lives and yours. You will be practicing cultural proficiency and racial literacy while learning strategies for culturally proficient instruction.

In thinking about our journey, I visualized how the steps might look on a flowchart. The following flowchart illustrates the path of our journey.

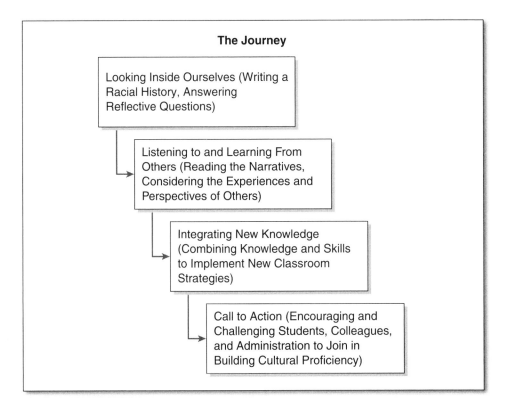

Even though the illustration is simple, the topic is complex. Due to the complexity of the material, I offer the following disclaimers as I take this journey with you.

DISCLAIMERS

I am an antiracist, yet I must remember, "even antiracist educators reproduce a racialized social system" (Pollock, 2008, p. 348). I have no other choice; I am part of this system. To continue this work, I pledge to do my best and work within this unequal system to try and change it. This book is my attempt to do that, but it is only what *I know I know* at this time in my life.

This book is a journey to learn about mixed-identity students; it is not designed as a handbook of classroom instruction. Cultural proficiency is "*not* a set of independent activities or strategies you learn to use with others" (Terrell & Lindsey, 2009, p.21). Even though there are strategies for the classroom embedded at the end of the chapters as well as an entire chapter, Chapter 9, devoted to classroom strategies, the focus is on change as an *inside-out* process. This inside-out process is the "first step in one's personal transformation that can lead to systemic educational reform" (Terrell & Lindsey, 2009, p. 3). We begin with our racial autobiographies and continue our journey from the inside to the outside as the model reflects.

I prefer the term *mixed identity* because it eliminates the term *race*, which is a debatable term in the research. Throughout the book, the terms are used interchangeably since they are interchanged in many of the articles and books written on the topic. Also, in some cases, the labels for identities and *races* are capitalized and in other cases they are not, based on the context and the sources of the information.

Finally, the writers of the narratives occasionally use capitalization and grammatical constructions that may differ from the preferred Corwin style. These constructions remain in order to retain the integrity, individuality, and voice of the narrator.

As you journey through this book, you will read personal narratives of those who contributed their stories. Without these, there would be no book. These individuals share very personal aspects of their lives.

I hope you gain as much from your journey with the book as I did in mapping it for you.

1

Beginning the Journey

Welcome to our journey to understand better the multiracial students who walk through our classroom doors. By choosing to read this book, you're expressing your interest in learning more about them.

What interests you about multiracial students?

_____

_____

_____

_____

Your response above sets a goal for your learning, and your interest takes you on a journey to learn what you *don't know you don't know*, opening your mind to learning about the experiences of those who are not like you. This is necessary for educators in a diverse classroom where oftentimes relationships fail to develop due to a lack of under-standing between teachers and students. Terrell and Lindsey, in *Culturally Proficient Leadershi*p (2009), state "educators and students treat one another differently because of the lack of shared experiences" (p. 9). If there is a lack of shared experiences, how do we learn about each other? How do we share our experiences? One way is through our stories, and in this book you will read the stories of students, educators, and others whose stories differ from your own. By reading and sharing lived experiences, hopefully we can bridge differences and create powerful relationships that sustain learning.

I am aware that students who identify as belonging to more than one race share experiences that differ from my experiences. As an educator, I am interested in learning what those experiences might be and how I can better understand and support these students. I am on a journey to learn *what I don't know I don't know* about race. As you take this journey with me, I will make explicit my thinking and ask you to reflect upon your own.

I must offer a disclaimer here since my experience has been limited in the following ways: I was born and raised in the Midwest and taught 30 years in public schools there. Even though I was an active member of the International Education Consortium and traveled abroad to study African literature, it wasn't until the past several years that I actively worked with educators and students outside the Midwest region. Therefore, my journey involves more interaction with African Americans than with any other ethnic group except my own white culture. It also means my knowledge base is limited about many of the diverse cultures that compose our country. With that being said, I do believe that my journey offers you an opportunity to examine racial issues that plague our educational system and society. I offer what *I know I know* and suggest the means for you to learn and do the same.

HOW DO WE BEGIN THE JOURNEY TO UNDERSTAND RACE?

Our journey to understand race begins by thinking, writing, and looking at our own racial histories and by sharing them with others. Ideally, we will share our stories with colleagues and build a trusting community of educators with whom to travel this road. If you are in a school district not quite ready to do that, you can continue your own journey with the help of this book and others. But we have to do our own work. In *Courageous Conversations About Race,* Glenn Singleton and Curtis Linton (2006) state that we "cannot talk about race collectively as a nation, family, or school until we have individually talked about race in our own lives—personally, locally, and immediately" (p. 76). The following is an attempt to be personal, local, and immediate about my racial history, and I invite you to do the same with yours. My children, Leah and Reeve, share their stories and so does Brenda, the mother of my grandbaby.

RACIAL HISTORY

Think back over your life. Can you think of the first time you were aware of racial identity?

_____

_____

_____

_____

My first awareness of racial identity occurred when I entered the school bus on the first day of kindergarten. The first person I saw was Lloyd, the man who drove the bus to kindergarten. Lloyd did not look like me. My parents called Lloyd a "Negro." This is my first memory of people being identified by others based on physical features such as skin color.

My first memory was positive, and I saw Lloyd as a trusted adult who took care of me. However, just having the children call him "Lloyd" rather than Mr. Williams may have bestowed on us a liberty we would not have taken if he were white. I seriously doubt that black children of the 1950s in this small Southeast Missouri town would have been allowed to have called a white bus driver by his first name.

When I think about my racial history, I, as this white person, begin to think of the presence of people of color in my life; for I don't think of my "whiteness" as having a "racial history" without the presence of color. You may or may not do the same.

I outline my history in contrast to those who don't look like me rather than in comparison to those who do. I do this because—to me—my racial history is about my presence within the environment of whiteness until a person of color enters that environment.

Lloyd is the only nonwhite person with whom I recall interacting until I entered eighth grade. That winter in 1958, Cecil, a black male, joined our class during basketball season. One night after a victory, the coach took the team and the class supporters to the Southern Café. When they would not serve our star player, the coach stood up and marched us out the door. This experience was my first encounter with discrimination. I remember standing in the kitchen and telling my mom about the event, but I can't remember her reaction.

One black male attended my high school, and that was the extent of my experience, until college, with others I identify as belonging to a different racial group. In college I had a black girlfriend, but we were not close friends, and my entire social network was white and Christian. My life was extremely insular throughout my childhood and adolescence.

I married in college and lived for the next decade in the suburbs of St. Louis. My daughter, Leah, was born in 1969, and she entered her parents' world where our church was White, our schools were White, our neighborhoods were White, and our lives were White. I assumed my husband was monoracial, but at some point, Leah's grandparents informed us that her great-grandmother was Cherokee.

Leah shares her story:

Leah Ancona, White/Cherokee Indian, Born 1969
Bonnie Davis' Daughter
Architect, St. Louis, Missouri
Written narrative

When my mom first asked me to write for her book on mixed-racial heritage, I wasn't sure if I wanted to because I wasn't sure I really fit with her topic. You see, when I was a child, my mom told me I was part Indian, feather-not-dot.

I remember this from when I was about eight or nine, and the only experience I had with Indians at that time was Tonto from the Lone Ranger, which I watched faithfully each morning before school. Tonto was so cool. He had a pretty horse named Scout; he rode with the Lone Ranger; and he got kidnapped a lot, but he always got away. Having never actually met an Indian, I thought he was pretty neat, and if I was like him, I figured I was lucky. When I told my friends I was an Indian, they weren't so sure, so I explained that I could prove it. You see, I have a birthmark on my arm that I had never seen on anyone else, so I told my friends it was my Indian mark. It proved that I wasn't like them. I was special.

Part of me always wanted to be a real *Indian. Because as I grew up, I knew I wasn't really Indian. My mom kind of looked Indian, which helped fuel my fantasy, but she told me it wasn't from her side. I didn't really relate to my dad, so I wasn't sure if he knew any Indians. I didn't. And I desperately wanted to. Around this same time, my mom met and married a black man, and I became black. Of course I didn't really, but my school was all white, and they wanted to stay that way, so when my new dad came to pick me up from school, it immediately got noticed. The only black person in my school was a girl my age who was adopted, and she had been at this school since first grade. I can only imagine how she was treated before I arrived in fourth grade, but I know she was the meanest person in the entire school to me. I think she felt she finally had someone to treat as she had been treated for being different. When my brother was born, I could not have been happier. I took him everywhere I could, and nothing would please me more than being able to tell people he was my brother. Let me tell you, we got some looks with this little boy, looking so much like his dad, hanging on to my hand and walking down the streets of white suburbia. He was special, and I loved it.*

At school, being treated black sort of sucked. My classmates called me names and took every opportunity to tease me about things I could not control. I was completely outcast from the popular group, and the one other girl I mentioned made it her mission to make me miserable. I knew when it was time to go to high school, I was going to find some place with some Black people so I could fit in, and that's just what I did. While all the other girls from my grade school went to the various all-white Catholic girls' schools in town, I had a friend who found one in the city that had 50% black people. Fifty percent! I was going there so I could be with people like me; the problem was that they weren't. They were all either black or white. What was I? I was white, Indian, or black, depending on the audience, and I had no idea what to check on the "race" box on the standardized tests. I only knew I wanted to be anything but "White" or "Caucasian" because I was special and those terms just didn't fit.

I actively pursued relationships with the black girls in my school, and they just didn't know what to think of me. They didn't know who this crazy little white girl from the burbs, who wanted to listen to their music and be a part of their group, was. I was the only white girl in the OABC (Organization for the Appreciation of Black Culture) and had fun dancing to The Time during the annual talent show. I figured the white people didn't want me because of the color in my family, so I didn't want them either. I wanted to be with a group who would want me, and I figured the black girls were my best bet. I had a father who was black and a brother who was half black, and surely, they would want me in their group. But they didn't. You see, I wasn't black. I didn't share a common history. I wasn't special like them.

As I started looking at colleges, I was told I could get scholarships if I told people about my Indian background. I contacted my grandparents I hadn't seen in years, and they wrote the history of their side of the family, as much as they knew, and told me about my family. A relative from the past married an Indian woman on the Trail of Tears, and they had children eventually leading to me. I really was part Indian. I really was special.

I threw myself into being Indian during college. I joined the Native American organizations on campus, becoming president of them both during some part of my college career. I went to conferences about Native Americans and met a ton of amazing people. I participated in PowWows and recruited for my school from the local Indian junior college. And then I started to learn the real American history. I learned what whites had done to the native people when they came to this country. I met Russell Means, and he told me about what it was like growing up "Indian" and fighting for his rights in American Indian Movement (AIM) in the 1970s. He explained how important it is for Indians to look Indian and be proud of their culture. He also told me I should not have cut my hair, a poor decision I made just before his visit, because American Indians wear their hair long and proud. And while I worked for seven years on Indian issues, I felt like a fraud. After all, I knew I was just a little bit Indian and was it really fair to take away from someone who needed more than I and was more than just a little Indian? Was I really special?

After I graduated college, I joined the work force, and while I had my Minority Engineering achievements on my resume, I did not present myself as anything other than white. Why would I? I looked white, and I didn't have to face the typical issues of people of color. I didn't feel it was right for me to use this side of my background as a way to get something extra. What I found was it was a whole lot harder being a woman in my profession than anything else. So today, I represent myself as who I am: White, Native American, woman, architect, brunette, short, and all the other things that make me who I am. I do have a mixed heritage, and I do fit within my mom's book after all, because I am not any one thing or any one identity. I am special.

What did you learn from Leah's story?

_____

_____

_____

_____

Leah describes the complexities she faced from the mixed heritages found in her family, and her racial history echoes complexities found in the narratives throughout this book. I seldom thought of Leah as having a mixed heritage; however, since there was proof enough for her to receive a scholarship based on her Cherokee heritage, I was happy to receive the college help at a time when I was a single mother and living on one teacher's salary.

My first marriage ended, and two years later I met and married a black man. I found his world to be very different from my own. Even though that is an extremely naïve statement, I had no reason to think otherwise until I became involved with him. Since I did not have black friends and taught in a school district with no diversity, I remained as isolated as in my childhood. I knew I needed to learn more.

My son, Reeve, was born in 1979, and soon I faced experiences I would have never known in my all-white world. In the hospital, the nurse marked "Caucasian" on my son's paperwork without asking. Weeks later, as I changed his diaper in a department store bathroom, a Black woman noticed the black and blue spot at the base of his spine and like a fortune-teller foretelling his future, she whispered ominously, "He must be biracial because he has the *mark.*" The mark disappeared, kinky hair replaced my son's straight birth hair, and his skin darkened as he grew. I was now the mother of a biracial child in my White world (paraphrased and quoted from pp. 45–48, *How to Teach Students Who Don't Look Like You: Culturally Relevant Teaching Strategies*, 2006).

As the mother of a biracial child, I wanted to learn all I could about what that meant for my child and for me. I also wanted to learn how my son felt about being identified as biracial. But mostly, I avoided that conversation as Reeve was growing up because I was uncomfortable with it. Instead, I resorted to taking Reeve to countless multicultural events, hoping these experiences would make him comfortable in his difference. Fortunately, Reeve has grown to be an intelligent, reflective man, and when I asked him to write a piece for this book, I hoped he would, but I respected his right to refuse. He sent me the following:

Reeve Emanuel Davis, Mixed African American/White, Born 1979
Bonnie Davis' Son
Government Employee, Washington, DC
Written narrative

I guess I don't think about it too, too much. I've been considered Black *basically my whole life, so it's something I've learned to adapt to. I'm guessing that is a common trait to all mixed people of any ethnicity or race—adapting. You learn to be black enough to be part of one category and white enough to be part of another (if that's what your mixture is). If you ask if this makes one schizophrenic, I would say no, just smarter and provides a good ability to improvise. This is not a new concept or strange whatsoever. Your average black or Latino is probably used to acting one way in the* corporate *world versus how they would act in the real world amongst friends and family.*

And then the term mixed. *What the hell does that mean? If you are half Irish and half Cuban, what are you? And why do certain groups of people get labeled that and others don't. For example—Black, White, Puerto-Rican, Asian. . . . Most Puerto Rican's are in fact of mixed heritage, but for some reason, their ethnicity is on par with other people's race. Why is that? If you look at a census form, many say* Hispanic *and are lined up among other racial categories. So could you not be a white Puerto Rican? And if you claim you are*

Hispanic, and your ancestors are from Spain, are Spanish people from Spain not considered Anglo Saxon or White like most other European groups?

Why even get lost in all that madness of labels? Most mixed people would say the best you can do is to be you because many people won't understand that you fall outside of the categories . . . seems to be a foreign concept to them.

Maybe it's for simplicity sake. Yes, I would say I'm black because I won't get quizzed on what my background is. And there's not always a lot of time to sit down and discuss this topic every time someone asks you, nor should you have to.

I'm not going to lie; I honestly think trying to find some commonality among other mixed people is a little bit of a lost cause. Interesting, yes, but I am going to see you as a person and not our common bond as being mixed. This is because I am almost sure the way you grew up and your background is different from mine. I think a lot of mixed people attempt to break down their background in order to better explain themselves to the world. ("Oh, my dad is German and Italian, and my mother is Haitian and Native American.) If I do this, it's out of interest of my background, but not so I can spew a long explanation at someone when asked, "What is your background?" Not remembering exactly what the question was (but the topic was race), my black friend once told me, "No, you're a nigga," as if to verify my racial category. I think that's pretty solid evidence of what I am physically perceived as, wouldn't you agree?

Overall, I would say I like it. I can get along or be accepted by almost anyone, and there are many places around the heterogeneous world where I blend right in. The challenge is being able to keep up the act. For example, I basically look like a light-skinned African American man. I bet I could go to a place, like say, Morocco, and blend in relatively well. However, my Arabic skills are nonexistent, and my French is only, "aussi, aussi." So maybe I would fit in if I were mute—but anyway, the moral is I think most mixed people would say it is an undeniably positive feeling to be around people who look like you and blend in. This is an experience that I felt in Brazil, a feeling of belonging, but guess what? I only speak "um puoco" of Portuguese, and people growing up there would have a completely different story growing up than I, so how do we relate?

The negative is that there is never complete satisfaction of belonging. You're a drifter, a gray space, a neutral color, not loud enough to offend anyone either which way.

What did you learn from Reeve's story?

_____

_____

_____

_____

Reeve's final two sentences tug at this mother's heart. The lack of belonging he writes about continues as a strong theme throughout the narratives found in this book.

LEARNING WHAT I DIDN'T KNOW I DIDN'T KNOW

Because I now felt a need to learn more about "what I didn't know I didn't know," I searched for mentors, books, and organizations to guide me. I worked with the Anti-Defamation League program, A World of Difference, and began to facilitate workshops for them in the 1980s.

The high school where I taught was desegregated in 1984, and the black students new to my classes taught me more about issues of race. I was able to observe incidents that my husband and these students experienced that had never happened to me as a white woman. In particular, I remember Donna's story. Partway through the first year of the desegregation program, a teacher brought Donna to me and asked if I, an English teacher, would proofread a letter she had written to the school board. I read her letter and wept. Donna described how she and the other students of color had been placed in remedial classes and were largely ignored by both teachers and students. This was a pivotal experience for me and caused me to become a teacher ally for the desegregation students. Through my work with the students, I continued to learn more of what I *didn't know I didn't know.*

Donna, described above, taught me more about racial identity. She identified as a biracial girl, and she often passed for white in classrooms of all white students. She described the difficulties she faced as she sat in a classroom where the students did not identify her as biracial and were willing to make disparaging remarks about the other desegregation students in her presence. She also felt she received privilege due to her appearance that the other students in this historical desegregation movement were denied. She felt guilty about this. Donna caused me to begin to think about issues of racial identity in more complex ways and how a system of privilege might be bestowed upon some students in our classrooms with or without our knowledge. Donna challenged my assumptions about multiracial students.

My assumptions continue to be challenged, and I am now privileged to be the grandmother of a child possessing multiple heritages with a skin color blend of all. Below is her mother's story:

Brenda Àlvarez, Mexi-Rican/Borimex, Born 1976
Bonnie Davis' Granddaughter's Mother
Senior Public Relations Specialist, National Education Association,
    Washington, DC
Written narrative

I'm the product of a Mexican mama and a Puerto Rican papa. I like to say I'm Mexi-Rican or a Borimex. I always thought that since I was made up of two ethnic groups, I would be in a position of large-scale acceptance amongst my people. However, when coming of age, this combination proved to be damaging to my self-perception.

My parents separated when my mama was two months pregnant with me. As a result, I grew up listening to her talk about how Puerto Ricans aren't nice people, how I should never bring a Puerto Rican kid to the house and, more important, I shouldn't tell people I'm Puerto Rican. My mama wasn't the only one who told me to stop telling folks I was Puerto Rican, but my brother as well. One day, my brother heard me tell a group of neighborhood White kids that I was Puerto Rican.

He immediately called me into the house. As soon as I walked in, he grabbed me by the shoulders and with tears in his eyes said, "Don't be telling people we're Puerto Rican! Don't you know White people don't like Puerto Ricans?!" As a little brown girl I never realized that other brown people belonged to other ethnic/racial groups.

Negative comments about being Puerto Rican were not just in my home but in the playground as well. At school, Mexican kids had no qualms about calling me a spic*. In fact, one day, a White kid called my girlfriend a* spic*. Her response to him was, "I ain't no spic. I'm not Puerto Rican." She then went on to explain to me that Puerto Ricans are spics, and Mexicans are wetbacks. I remained silent.*

I carried this silence with me for years. Instead of telling people to go to hell, I accepted their word as truth. I began to loathe the very idea of my Puerto Rican blood. I felt wrong. I felt negative. Soon enough, I stopped telling people I was Puerto Rican. Puerto Rican kids weren't as offensive. They were just less inclusive because I didn't speak like them; I didn't live in a predominantly Puerto Rican neighborhood, or I didn't look *Puerto Rican.*

During my junior high and high school years, I stifled my voice because I didn't know where I belonged. However, I eventually rediscovered myself during my late college years. I exposed myself not just to Puerto Rican culture but also to all cultures. The more I stepped outside of my comfort zone, the more I was able to close the gap of my identity crisis. I eventually capped my insecurities after a trip to the island where I met my papa. After 24 years, the mystery of who and what made me was sealed the instant I saw my eyes on his face.

I now look at the whopping eyes of my five-month-old daughter, Eva Salomé Álvarez Davis. She is Mexican; she is Puerto Rican; she is White; and she is Black. Yet, when I look at her, I don't see any of this. All I see is a little girl who has the potential to enjoy life and to develop her own thoughts; I see a little girl who will be confident in her skin regardless of ethnic and racial backgrounds; and I see a little girl who will benefit from being multicultural and who will cross all boundaries despite color and language.

I'm excited to be her mama.

What did you learn from Brenda's story?

_____

_____

_____

_____

The above narratives share some of the blended histories in my family. Now, it is time to think about your own.

Write about the first time you met someone with a different racial identity than your own.

_____

_____

_____

_____

Write about a family member or other loved one who has a different racial identity than yours.

_____

_____

_____

_____

Since we are on a journey to understand how mixed-race identity operates within the context of racial classification and plays out in our classrooms, writing our racial histories is critical to our understanding. In writing our racial histories and keeping them personal, local, and immediate, we lay the groundwork for a continued journey to racial literacy. It offers us the process and the product to challenge our assumptions about others, and in this case, multiracial students. Since this book focuses on multiracial students, ultimately, we are searching to better understand the multiracial experience.

That all sounds fine, yet there is a warning we must heed. We have to continually balance the information we learn, whether from the research or from the personal narratives, with the temptation to use it to form stereotypes about multiracial students and other students of color. There is no single multiracial experience, for if there were, a stereotype could aptly describe it. But there is not. There is no singular white experience, and if there were, a stereotype could describe it. If you are white, you know you are not like every other white person in this country. The same can be said about students of color, and, in this case, multiracial students of color. In _Challenging Multiracial Identity_ (2006), Rainier Spencer states "there is no singular interracial experience any more than there is any singular Afro-American or any singular Euro-American experience" (p. 19). When I draw singular conclusions about the multiracial experience, I create stereotypes and deny the richness and variety of each of the narratives included in this book.

One such narrative comes from Donna Rogers Beard, who shares another grandmother's story:

> _Three facts that will liberate the so-called biracial child and the rest of us: One, there is no such thing as race. Two, life is difficult. Three, culture, as we know it, is too narrowly defined. I am the grandmother of a so-called mixed-race or interracial child. I want her to grow up in a world that has put race on the shelf with the belief that the world is flat._

Like me, Donna Rogers Beard has solidified her thinking about race with the birth of her granddaughter. She writes,

> _It has taken me nearly 60 years to understand and clarify my rejection of race as a legitimate category. The birth, two years ago, of my granddaughter_

has caused me to focus on the topic of racial identity. I hope that I will be able to share with my granddaughter the following: There is no such thing as race. She can save herself a whole lot of grief if she does not allow herself to be sucked into this false construct. She must take control of her world by understanding who she is—what does she enjoy doing, who does she enjoy being with, and why—and not allow anyone to tell her that she must identify with any group or person based on what society has defined as race.

Even though there is no singular racial experience for a group, we each have a singular racial history or story that we can tell. Your story differs from mine and from Donna's, and it is just as valid and important. By writing our own stories and using them as the basis for our understanding others' stories, we can learn more about ourselves and the shared experiences of those who do not look like us.

Recall your first encounter with racial discrimination. Write about it below.

_____

_____

_____

_____

Describe your school years. What encounters did you have with others who did not look like you?

_____

_____

_____

_____

Describe your young adult years. What encounters did you have with persons from other racial identity backgrounds?

_____

_____

_____

_____

What life experiences caused you to look more closely at issues of race?

_____

_____

_____

_____

Describe any pivotal experiences you have had with students.

_____

_____

_____

_____

What are your assumptions about multiracial students?

_____

_____

_____

_____

Below are some things I now know. Please add your new understandings to the growing list.

WHAT I LEARNED

- A racial history has to be personal, local, and immediate (Singleton and Linton, 2006).
- As a white person, I have not had to make choices about what box to check on forms. I knew I was white.
- I always felt the white box was the only box to check, and unconsciously or consciously, I believed it to be the best box.
- My racial history as a white person is written in contrast to persons of color.
- There is a system of privilege based on phenotypes or physical appearance.
- Multiracial students complicate our understandings of race.
- "There is no singular interracial experience any more than there is any singular Afro-American or any singular Euro-American experience" (Spencer, 2006, p. 19).
- Learning the stories of others builds my knowledge base to better understand my students.

What have you learned? Write about some things you know now.

_____

_____

_____

_____

Exploring my racial history grounds my thinking for the next steps on our journey.

TAKING IT TO THE CLASSROOM: STRATEGIES TO BUILD COMMUNITY AND IMPROVE ACHIEVEMENT

- Have students write a _bio_ poem—a poem that expresses their uniqueness. Post the poems on the walls of your classroom.
- Create a _Visual Buffet_ of pictures on the walls of your schools. Ensure the school walls are covered with pictures of students of many different colors and cultures. Even though this is a well-known strategy, I still find bare walls when I walk into schools.
- Build a classroom library with books about students with diverse heritages (see suggestions at the end of the chapter).
- If you are an English teacher or an elementary teacher, use a writers' workshop format so that students write their own cultural histories.

OUR JOURNEY THUS FAR

We are building background knowledge as we continue our journey to learn more about multiracial students. In Chapter 2, we begin "falling off the cliff" to learn more about _what we don't know we don't know_ about race and how racism weaves its way through every aspect of our lives, including issues of identity that impact our students in today's classrooms. Since there is no singular racial group experience, our journey takes a detour as we look more closely at issues of race.

SUGGESTED RESOURCES FOR WRITING CULTURAL AND RACIAL HISTORIES

Davis, B. (2006). _How to teach students who don't look like you: Culturally relevant teaching strategies._ Thousand Oaks, CA: Corwin.

Singleton, G., & Linton, C. (2006). _Courageous conversations about race: A field guide for achieving equity in schools._ Thousand Oaks, CA: Corwin.

Terrell, R., & Lindsey, R. (2009). _Culturally proficient leadership: The personal journey begins within._ Thousand Oaks, CA: Corwin.

2

What Is Race?

In Chapter 1, we wrote and reflected upon our racial histories and established a context for continuing our journey to understand the impact of race. We described the racial lens through which we see the world. With this understanding, we can move to the question, *What is race?* This question has haunted me for decades. Even though I used to identify people as fitting into different races, I never understood exactly why or how. I have always wanted to better understand exactly what race *is* and how the concept of race evolved.

Originally, I thought race had only to do with physical appearance. It wasn't until I began to study the phenomenon of race that I learned about its anthropological, economic, sociological, and political aspects. The concept of race is so complicated, and I continue to search for better definitions and more understanding.

What is your understanding of race?

_____

_____

_____

_____

Early on, I thought of race as a simple classification system that put humans into distinct categories based mostly on skin color and a few other physical features. In geography class in elementary school, I learned about the *races* of the world. But as I grew older, simple observation about skin color caused me to realize it could not be a sole determiner of race. **S**kin color varies tremendously within every racial designation—when I have a tan, my skin color is darker than many people who self-identify or are identified by others as being "people of color." So if it is not skin color, I wondered if there were other physical features distinctive to race. The answer is no. There is no distinctive characteristic that defines one as belonging to a certain race.

THEN WHAT IS *RACE?*

People hold varied beliefs about the definition of *race*. Some believe race is a biological reality attached to a variety of physical features (phenotypes). Others believe race is the socially constructed meaning attached to a variety of physical features (phenotypes). Still others say race does not exist at all, but it is rather the *belief* in either of these.

Are any of these correct? What do you think?

_____

_____

_____

_____

The American Anthropological Association has been studying race for some time, and it issued a statement on race in the 1990s to help clarify erroneous definitions.

AMERICAN ANTHROPOLOGICAL ASSOCIATION'S STATEMENT ON RACE

The American Anthropological Association's Statement on Race (1998) states that "we have been conditioned to viewing human races as natural and separate divisions within the human species based on visible physical differences" (p. 8). However, this is simply not true. Due to the scientific expansion of the 20th century, it has "become clear that human populations are not unambiguous, clearly demarcated, biologically distinct groups" (p. 2). So the American Anthropological Association says that there are *no* distinct biological groups we can define as races.

Do you agree or not? Explain.

_____

_____

_____

_____

How does the American Anthropological Association know there are no such things as distinct biological groups we can define as races? The American Anthropological Association says it knows this because physical traits—such as hair texture, skin color, and physical features—are inherited independently. These physical traits are known as *phenotypes*. Phenotypes are the visible characteristics of an organism resulting from the interaction between its genetic makeup and the environment.

Interestingly, one trait does not predict the presence of others. Dark skin may be associated with kinky hair or wavy or straight hair. All of these combinations are found among people in tropical areas (American Anthropological Association [AAA], 1998). Since phenotypes are inherited independently, they cannot be bound together to be indicators of distinct groups of people known as racial categories. Yet they *are* bound together when used for racial profiling. Racial profiling, the practice of categorizing individuals based on phenotypes associated with particular *racial* categories, continues today even with scientific evidence to the contrary. For example, racial profiling occurs when we target persons who *appear* to be members of the same race. Remember how persons who *looked* Middle Eastern to some people may have been profiled as terrorists following the September 11, 2001 terrorist attack in the United States.

In *Philosophy of Science and Race*, Naomi Zack (2002), now professor of philosophy at the University of Oregon, underscores the lack of evidence for the existence of race. She states, "Differences in skin tone are gradual, not discrete; and blood-type variations occur independently of the more visible phenotypes associated with race, such as skin color and hair texture" (p. 88). There are not different blood types associated with different races. The same blood types run through all our veins, no matter our racial categories. Furthermore, Zack states that "essences, geography, phenotypes, genotypes, and genealogy are the only known candidates for physical scientific bases of race. Each fails. Therefore, there is no physical, scientific basis for the social racial taxonomy" (p. 88).

If there are no distinct biological groups we can define as races, then what are we? The American Anthropological Association (AAA) states that we are truly a human race, not distinct races. We all belong to the same species. The AAA says we have continued to share genetic material that has maintained all of humankind as a single species, not distinct races. Learning this was a huge *a-ha* for me. I assumed that brown and black people, because of their skin color, belonged to a different race than I, a white person, belonged to, but I now know we all belong to a single race: the human race.

Reflect upon this information. What are your thoughts?

_____

_____

_____

_____

Donna Rogers Beard, an award-winning Advanced Placement (AP) history teacher (and grandmother who shared her thoughts in Chapter 1), has studied issues of race her entire teaching career. Her thoughts on race follow:

> Race *was defined one law at a time in the United States. If we were separate races, we would not be able to mate. Welcome to a new day. No species on earth is as biologically close as the human species. The world is round, and there is only one race—the human race. In the late 20th century, the human genome project revealed that humans cannot be biologically classified into races. We are one race.* Newsweek's *December 4, 1995 issue explored the topic thoroughly. PBS has an incredible three-part series that can be previewed at http://www.pbs.org/race/000_General/000_00-Home.htm.*
>
> *To my granddaughter and all other humans, I say welcome to the 21st century. Embrace it. Get to know yourself; reject the category of race as a way of defining who you are. Know that life is difficult for all us humans. Enjoy the many good days ahead of you that you will have when you are in control of who you are.*

If we agree with Donna that there is no such thing as race, how did the concept evolve? Race evolved as a mode of classification linked to colonization that was used to rationalize attitudes and treatment by those in power (AAA, 1998, p. 4) and for economic power. In the United States, leaders among the European Americans linked "superior traits with Europeans and negative and inferior ones to blacks and Indians" (p. 4), thereby institutionalizing and deeply embedding these beliefs in the American psyche. There was a need for the belief in race, for how else could we enslave fellow human beings? If we believed some people belonged to an inferior race, it justified the treatment. Unfortunately, we still see these beliefs in and assumptions about race played out on our national scene and in our neighborhoods, schools, and families.

Karen Notarainni, wife and mother, saw assumptions about race play out in her family when they adopted a child while living in Brazil:

> *Only several days after we'd spread the happy news of our new parenthood status did we encounter our first incident. My father asked, "What color is she?" I responded that she is the color we get after four or five days in the sun. When Alicia was 10 months old, we moved home to south Florida. This is when my real diversity training began.*

She is now used to encountering people's assumptions about race as the mother of a child whose phenotypes do not match hers.

> *Once, I was asked by a child in the grocery store line if I was the babysitter. Other times, I felt eyes inspecting my daughter and me. Many people commented on how beautiful her coloring was. The black woman in the grocery store said Alicia was beautiful and looked just like her granddaughter.*

Black people were especially complimentary of Alicia then. When she started talking, Alicia would tell me that she was uncomfortable that people were looking at her. And they were. Sometimes, I knew the stares were because she was an exceptionally beautiful child. Other times, people stared with more menacing thoughts—wondering if I wildly or stupidly crossed the racial divide in my sexual history. To Alicia, I always explained that people were admiring how beautiful she was or how pretty she looked in a particular outfit or her new sunglasses. As the Hispanic population grew rapidly in south Florida, this attention diminished somewhat. South Americans seemed to recognize Alicia as some version of Latina.

At this point, it becomes relevant to explain that we have practiced avoiding classifying our daughter in terms of race. Alicia's birth mother is of fair complexion and has wavy hair. It is likely from Alicia's physical features that she is of mixed race, but we don't know that for sure. Also, matters of race are treated differently in the United States than they are in Brazil. For example, Portuguese contains many more words for various shades of skin color than English and places less emphasis on race outright. Contrarily, F. James Davis' book, titled Who is Black? One Nation's Definition, *outlines how "the one drop rule" was used in the United States' legal system as the basis for determining a person's race. Since blacks could not own property in post-Civil War times, "the one drop rule" was the legal basis on which to deprive the offspring of wealthy landowners and their slaves of any entitlement to property inheritance, funneling the wealth to the recognized members of these aristocratic families. Lineage and prosperity were inexorably linked at that time. There could be an argument that they still are. As I grew to understand these principles, I feared for my daughter. I believed that her being considered South American was preferable to being identified as black because of challenging race relations even now in the United States. Surprisingly, many white people with whom I am acquainted don't quickly grasp the difference between race and nationality.*

Reflect on what Karen says. Write your thoughts below.

_____

_____

_____

_____

If there is scientific proof that race does not exist, why do we still treat others based on our perceptions of the racial categories to which they belong? In addition to phenotypes, the answer may lie in behaviors. As the concept of *race* evolved as a worldview, behaviors were attributed to different groups, and culture was implied to be genetically inherited. What we might label as *race* is really *cultural*, and the judgments we often make about others that we attribute to race are judgments about their cultural behaviors. Therefore, cultural behaviors are being inappropriately defined as racial behaviors. Race is implying biological designation, and culture is something else.

Culture is the totality of ideas, beliefs, values, activities, and knowledge of a group or individuals who share historical, geographical, religious, linguistic, ethnic, or social traditions and who transmit, reinforce, and modify those traditions. Put more simply, culture is everything you learned by growing up in a particular context, and it results in a set of expectations for appropriate behavior in seemingly similar contexts. Culture, not race, defines our behaviors, and our culture provides us with a map for living that offers consistency and predictability in our everyday actions. Cultural expectations help us to keep outsiders outside and insiders controlled, thereby sustaining our group culture (Terrell & Lindsey, 2009). Ethnic cultures are groups of people "united by ancestry, language, physiology, and history, as well as by the beliefs and practices" (Robins, Lindsey, R. B., Lindsey, D. B., & Terrell, 2002, p. 52).

Our group or ethnic culture is learned, and "it is a basic tenet of anthropological knowledge that all normal human beings have the capacity to learn any cultural behavior" (American Anthropological Association [AAA], 1998, p. 7). We learn the cultural behaviors of the groups in which we were socialized.

Think about cultural behaviors you learned as a child. Write about them.

_____

_____

_____

_____

I learned the cultural behaviors of Catholicism as a child, and I mastered the practice of being a Catholic. If all Catholics had green hair, would I have been classified as belonging to a _race_ of Catholics? Yet this happens with race.

Mani Barajas, a young man whose mother is of Mexican heritage and whose father is African American, shares that he is often told, "You don't act Black," or "You don't act Mexican." He understands that his peers are referring to cultural behaviors, not racial designations, but it irritates him that others assume he should act a certain way because of his skin color.

While teaching, I found that I had to fight not to assign racial labels to cultural behaviors. Students from different cultural groups may behave differently than students from other cultural groups. Yet it was so easy to group students based on skin color rather than culture, too often forgetting that students of color come to our classrooms from hundreds of different cultures, not as homogeneous races.

Have you assigned racial labels to cultural behaviors? Is this something you might do because you "don't know you don't know"? Reflect below.

_____

_____

_____

_____

When I'm trying to better understand the impact of race on my assumptions, I often turn the question around. Rush Limbaugh accused Colin Powell of supporting Barack Obama in the presidential race because they shared the same *race;* however, no one accused Rush Limbaugh of supporting John McCain because they share the same race. We can sometimes test our racist assumptions by simply switching the scenario and asking if it would occur in the same way if both parties were white.

Race is sometimes used interchangeably with *culture,* and the confusion deepens. According to Singleton and Linton (2006) in *Courageous Conversations About Race,* culture describes "how we live on a daily basis in terms of our language, ancestry, religion, food, dress, musical tastes, traditions, values, political and social affiliations, and recreation" (pp. 169–70). What we may call *race* when we observe individuals acting a certain way may be behaviors they learned within a cultural framework. Race, for the most part, is the meaning "affixed to the melanin content found in the skin, hair, and eyes" (p. 170); therefore, persons with a lot of melanin are defined as being "of color," and those with little are defined as white. Race both *exists* and *does not exist* in the United States and throughout the Western world and "racial issues are not about physical skin color but rather stem from the meaning and value people assign to skin color" (p. 106). The meaning people assign to skin color is based on a system of power and superiority. Race as a biological reality does not exist, but as stated above, race both exists and does not exist in our everyday lives because people assign meaning and value to others based on phenotypes. Therefore race is based on power and superiority, and culture and ethnicity are based on common heritages.

The American Anthropological Association concludes "present-day inequalities between so-called 'racial' groups are not consequences of their biological inheritance but products of historical and contemporary social, economic, educational, and political circumstances" (AAA, 1998, p. 8). These present-day inequalities can impact the mixed students and may affect their perceptions of themselves and how they fit into the culture in which they live.

Think about what the term race means to you. How does the above information challenge and/or change your thinking? Share below.

_____

_____

_____

_____

Following are additional narratives from individuals who self-identify racially in different ways or reject the notion of race altogether. Please read and reflect on the following narratives as you continue to discover your own meaning for race.

Donna Rogers Beard, Human Race, Born 1946
Distinguished History Teacher, Clayton School District,
** Clayton, Missouri**
Written narrative

In 1967, I was forced to speak out on the issue of race mixing. *That year, the Warren Court was considering the Loving v. Virginia case that struck down the anti-miscegenation laws. I was the only person of color in a political science class of over 300 students. The professor presented the case to the class and invited comments. I seldom spoke out in any of my classes at Illinois State University. I was often the only person of color in the class. In addition, as a history major and political science minor, I was often one of few females. I could not believe the opinions voiced by almost everyone who spoke to the subject of miscegenation.*

They supported the laws because race mixing was bad. The worst comments said miscegenation was bad because it produced people who had physical and mental problems. More enlightened students said that they felt government should not legislate who anyone should marry, but in reality the offspring of such a union would not be accepted by either race. Those children would have miserable lives. I had to speak out. In a few minutes, I had to give a cogent, concise, strong statement that would hopefully cause my classmates to think rationally about race. *I told them that most* black *people they knew were of mixed race. At that time, I too believed in race. I felt my freckled face burning as I told them that black people came in many shades, from blonde, blue-eyed complexions to ebony black. We were of varying mixtures of white, black, and red. We were the face of America. Few of us were purely Negroid. I named Lena Horne, Thurgood Marshall, Walter White, Frederick Douglass, and every notable black person I could who was light brown to white in color. The black community was used to black folks of every color possible. Several people came up to me after class and said that I had given them something to think about. My professor thanked me for speaking up.*

In 1981, I read a book that gave me a powerful tool that I have shared with my son, my students, and anyone who complains about the problems of life. The book is The Road Less Traveled, *published in 1978 by psychiatrist M. Scott Peck. I was going through a rather difficult time in my life. My marriage was coming apart, and I had returned to the classroom after a three-year absence. I still struggled with being seen as the Oreo, the sell-out, not black enough by adults and too many black students. The first line of that book became my mantra. He began with the line that life is difficult. That if you accept the fact that life is difficult, you will find life much easier. This life was never meant to be easy. When you face difficult times you say, "This is life." When you have happy times, you rejoice at your good fortune. He then goes on to give excellent advice on how to minimize the difficult times with a disciplined approach.*

What does this revelation that life is difficult have to do with miscegenation? I will share with my granddaughter, as I have shared with anyone who will listen, that growing up in my all black community in Chicago and attending my all black schools, I had a hell of a time as a child. I was bullied almost every day in elementary school. I was skinny, tall, freckled-faced, and I wore glasses. I was what people today define as a nerd. My mother kept me in oxford shoes that were good for my feet and insisted that I wear braids until I was in seventh grade. I lived in a house full of adults; therefore, I was not that comfortable with my peers. I escaped into a world of books. As a result, I had a vocabulary and way of speaking that did not make my peers comfortable with me. Also, I was a teacher's pet.

Strangely, I was popular with most of the kids in my class and neighborhood but the target of the bullies. Adolescence was often painful. I matured late. Painfully skinny, with a stick shape at a time when being an hour glass, stacked girl was important made for a difficult high school social life until my sophomore year. At the end of my freshman year, my parents decided to make life even more difficult for me by moving the family to the outskirts of a small, nearly all-white town in northeastern Ohio. We joined the only other black person there, my mother's cousin. There we lived for six months. I was the first black student in the school system. It was 1959, and just one year before, Governor Faubus of Arkansas had closed down the state's schools to avoid integration. I was taunted almost everyday on the school bus. One courageous girl, with whom I correspond to this day, stood by me. She and I had lunch together every day. She walked me to the school bus and invited me to attend away football games with her family. She was my only guest at my 15th birthday party. Most students were cordial. They spoke. A few ate with us on occasion. On the bus, my next-door neighbor often sat with me and endured the racial slurs that were often hurled my way by the bullies.

It did not take long for me to realize what a favor my parents had done me. I spent those months as an observer. I watched white children exhibit much of the same behavior I had seen throughout my school experience. There were the cliques, the mean girls, and the bullies. Seating in the cafeteria at both my Chicago and Ohio high school was segregated by interest groups. The jocks and the cheerleaders sat separated by gender but close to each other. The choir and music kids sat together. And there I sat in both schools with the rather independent square girls who loved to talk books and movies. I left Galion, Ohio, with a new understanding about life. It would take Peck's book years for me later to validate what I had learned; life was difficult everywhere for everyone. For some it was even more difficult.

What I brought to the integrated settings of college and my career, as a teacher, was an understanding that one had to look at human behavior and not racial behavior. Of course there was a possibility that one was rejected as the cheerleader because of race, but there was no guarantee that if one were at a school where everyone was of the same race, that life would go the way you wanted it to turn out. There were isappointments and success that would be there because that is what happens to us humans as we go through life.

Donna's narrative offers a powerful journey toward understanding race. What did you learn from her words?

_____

_____

_____

_____

Karen Hayes, Baby Boomer, African American/White/Blackfoot Native American
Associate Professor, Department of Educational Administration and Supervision University of Nebraska, Omaha, Nebraska
Written narrative

I am the first born of four siblings. I was born in Sioux City, Iowa. As a child we moved to St. Louis, Missouri, where I resided until I was nine. We then moved to Chicago, Illinois, until my senior year of high school. We then were relocated to Omaha, Nebraska, where I attended the University of Nebraska. My father started out working in the meat packing industry. He was a very smart man, and the Department of Agriculture offered him a position as a meat inspector. He began pursuing his college degree; I remember Daddy going to school and working throughout my entire life. It was his desire to provide a better life for his family and why he continued to stay in school. I believe it took him 15-plus years to finish his degree in chemistry; he then became a chemist for the United States Department of Agriculture. I offer this background for you to understand the importance of education that was placed on our family. I remember my paternal grandmother telling me that she would not attend my wedding unless I had a college degree. I remember working very hard to finish my degree in May as I was planning for a June wedding!

My maternal grandmother was Irish and African American. My maternal grandfather was Blackfoot Native American and African American. My paternal grandparents were African American. I identified with my African American heritage the most because that is the ethnicity that I was exposed to. My mother didn't speak much about our Native American heritage, and I did not know what questions to ask. Even as an adult, I have not been able to totally embrace that part of myself . . . I feel a desire to seek greater knowledge in that part of my history. I have always been proud of being an African American. I know that has nothing to do with society and everything to do with my family's love.

Society tries to box us in. Society makes assumptions by how we look on the outside. My mother has been told that she looks Italian. My dad has been told that he looks Cuban. I've been told that I look Ethiopian. My children have been told that they look Hispanic. All of these statements are based on what people see on the outside. We as a society are judgmental and stereotypical based on outward appearances.

I remember never seeing a person of color on television and never having a doll to love that looked like me. Through family and teachers, I learned to love myself anyway.

At the end of third grade, I remember moving to Chicago; we lived in a predominately African American community. Looking back on that experience, I know that we were poor; however, as a child, I didn't ever feel a lack. I know we lived on the second floor of a home with our landlord on the first floor and additional neighbors on the third floor. I also realized that I had one dress-up dress, and when I did get a new outfit for Easter, it was because my paternal grandmother made it for me. I also knew that I never went to the beauty shop; whenever my hair was pressed, it was once again because of my paternal grandmother who would stand over the stove with a hot comb and press my hair until it shined!

Omaha, Nebraska, is where I experienced a culture shock. For the first time, we lived in an all-white neighborhood. My parents weren't sure where to find a diverse neighborhood, so we settled where we were able to find suitable, affordable housing in a safe neighborhood within a new city. We made friends quickly. However, for the first time, I was able to understand that some people may not want to associate with me or like me . . . not because they knew me but because they didn't want to know me because of the color of my skin.

As a family, however, I believe we flourished. Dad had his degree and was head of a laboratory for the Department of Agriculture. Mom started growing in her profession and began advancing her education. She started working in insurance and human resources and was very successful. I was a university student and became a part of campus sit-ins for equity on campus. I became an advocate for equality and social justice.

Because of our activism on campus, I was able to be a part of a movement that eventually helped to create the Office of Multicultural Affairs and the departments for Black studies, Native American studies, and Women studies. I felt that I was helping to make our community a better place to live for all of its citizens. I am very proud of the active role I played at the university, and I am reminded of that role 35 years later as I serve as one of the first African American professors in the Department of Educational Administration and Supervision at the university where I began.

Joe Rousseau, Oo'henumpa Lakota/Cherokee/Irish/German, Born 1971
Teacher, Middle School Science, Lincoln, Nebraska
Written narrative

I have asked my grandfather for his help in relating my story to you. During college, while taking History and Culture of the Native American, I was encouraged to visit my reservation for the first time. My grandfather's sister, Grandma Charlotte, welcomed my dog and me warmly. I learned much about my grandfather and myself. I learned he was an excellent storyteller. This is why I have asked him for assistance with my story even though he passed away when I was in the Navy.

My parents married on November 11, 1967, Veterans' Day. My father finished out his tour in Vietnam and his enlistment in the Navy, and they moved to Quartz Hill, California. I have been told by my mother that they wanted kids but were having trouble getting pregnant. They were also having trouble with the marriage. Early in 1971, my mother became pregnant. She took this as a sign to continue with the marriage. I was born on December 2, 1971, in Lancaster, California. My parents moved around while my father chased his vocation of cowboying. He was often out of work, and we lived on my mother's nursing income.

I have been told that my mother left my father because he would not keep a job and spent all of our money at the bar. She did not want him driving drunk with me in the truck. So she left and moved to Norfolk, Nebraska. I was still an infant. I do not remember living with my father. He stayed clear all of my elementary school years and did not make an appearance until I graduated from high school in 1990. All I had to know him by were stories given to me by my mother. She spoke well about my father. She was honest about his drinking but did not put him down. I am grateful for my mother's strength and intelligence. I often think my father knew I was being cared for, and therefore, he did not need to be in my life during my childhood. I have learned that you take care of the children that are near you; my father was taking care of whichever child was near him.

I am named after my paternal grandfather, Joe Rousseau, and I have named my son after this same man. My grandfather is Lakota; his wife is Cherokee. This makes my father half Lakota, half Cherokee. My maternal grandfather is Irish, and his wife is German. My mother is Irish and German. This leaves me with an internal conflict. I know who my mother and father are, but who am I? I have always checked the Indian box; that is what my mother has instructed me to do. I attended a different school until the fifth grade. My mother and I moved within the town of Norfolk from one rented house or apartment to another, and then during second and third grade, we lived in Austin, Texas. During fourth grade, we came back to Nebraska, and I attended Northern Hills Public School.

Finally, in fifth grade, a doctor at the hospital where my mother worked offered to pay my tuition to attend Norfolk Catholic High School. I finished my education in this parochial system. I felt a little awkward having someone pay for my tuition and also coming from a single parent household. Adults would wrinkle their foreheads and say, "You poor little boy, without a father." I never understood where they were coming from. I had a father, and my uncle always attended the father-son picnics with me, so why did they pity me? There were not spaces for us to explore our identity attending this Catholic school. I remember a classmate I graduated with telling me that he realized I was an Indian when we were in high school. I always knew I was an Indian. I had the books to prove it, books with white authors talking about the savage, superstitious Indian. The books were filled with artificially posed pictures of Indians with war paint and feathers.

Growing up in Norfolk, a small town with around 25,000 people, has impacted my worldview. The town has changed over the years. Its diversity is increasing, and I have felt this change. In the beginning, the town's problems were placed upon the shoulders of the Indians; after the meat packing plant arrived, the blame went to the Mexicans. Currently it's the Sudanese fault. I hope someday this little town will start to look favorably towards diversity.

I get to hear overt racism, for when I am with my mother, I am viewed as white. I am "in the club," so to speak, and at times the conversation goes down the racist road. If I walk down the street with my father, then I am viewed as an Indian, and the racist conversation goes covert, but the message is still felt. It's interesting watching others' faces when they meet my father; it's different than when people meet my mother. I really notice this in restaurants.

I get to dance between two cultures, go from one to the next whenever I need to. I do feel the need to bring my father along to prove my Indianness to others. I am on the board at the Indian Center, president of the Lincoln Public School's Indian Parent Advisory Committee, secretary of the Nebraska Indian Education Association, and the staff sponsor of the Native American Caucus at the middle school where I teach. I have brought my father to each of these places so others will know I am Lakota. Why do I feel the need to bring my father to become accepted within these Native places?

Thankfully, I have found someone who knows this internal dilemma, someone who also has a brown parent and a white parent. A person I can talk to about this complexity whenever I need to. Cameya and I married this summer. I am fortunate to have met her on my journey through this world. Her perspective helps me navigate through the muddy waters of identity.

Identity is fluid and ever changing. As an educator, I feel my profession is fundamentally concerned with power, control, and identity. I strive to give this to the children I am blessed to spend time with each day in the classroom. As the educational philosopher John Dewey identifies in his book, Experience and Education, *it is the educator's role to create the conditions that provide the learner with the power and control, therefore facilitating each student's ability to form his and her own identity and not impose one.*

So who am I? Which box do I check? A couple of years ago, a student, who has one white parent and one black parent, put it very eloquently. He used the word mixed. I learn so much from the students I interact with each year. I like that word; I am mixed too. I am Joe Rousseau: an educator, a father, a son, a grandson, a human.

Thank you,

—Pilamayayelo

Joe says he dances between cultures. Describe what you think he means by that statement.

_____

_____

_____

_____

Michael Vaughn, Korean/White, Born 1979
High School History Teacher, St. Louis, Missouri
Written narrative

Childhood

I was born in Osan, South Korea, on October 11, 1979, in a world that had never known color or racism. The struggle of Koreans does not come from skin color, racism, or bigotry, but rather from gender. As a child, I have seen incidents that would make the United States—who am I kidding?—everyone disgusted or maybe even shed tears of sorrow and compassion. However, my life took a turn from that wretched world of gender inequality to an unknown world of America.

My mother told me that in America, you could be anything you want to be but that you had to work for it. Little did I know, as a young child, that there would be both physical and mental obstacles along the way. Coming from Korea, where racism was not an issue in the social stratosphere, in a way crippled me to what to expect to face in America. I got my first dose of reality as a young, non-English speaking foreigner during kindergarten. I wish that I could say that my experience in the American public school system was inviting, kind, and filled with love. However, only one word comes to mind—confused. I guess you could call me an easy target since I did not speak English or know a speck of any American customs, but racism and prejudice was my introduction to an "old, yet not so distant American custom." In this present time of 2007, being called "Chinese" doesn't bother me as much because of experiences and relationships I have acquired; however, as a six-year-old newcomer, that word was as devastating as using the "N" word to African Americans. In 1986, my first full year in American schools, the word Chinese started to clash with my life. Everyday for two or three months, another classmate would call me Chinese as a means to deteriorate my self-image. During that time, the physical mimicking of slanted eyes would even cause me some confusion and sadness to try to understand what that meant, especially when another minority caused that type of hurt.

The second dose of reality was that same year in which the same incident happened. After a few months, the harassment dwindled; however, another issue arose, not from another classmate, but from my teacher. To keep the story short, the classmate who had harassed me was an African American boy, and my teacher was African American as well. The incident came to a halt when my mother had a couple of words with that student one morning, and the conversation between my mother and the student made its way up the grapevine to my teacher. Once again, to keep the story short, there was no conference or mediation process setup by the guidance office; however, the teacher took it upon herself to announce to the class my mother had picked on "the black boy." From there on out, I was the troublemaker of the class and always the last one chosen for free time by the teacher. Needless to say, this would not be my last experience with racism.

Adolescence

My first full sense of belonging came with my family's move to England, where my father's career was with the Air Force. The great thing about military life is there were other kids like me who understood the same struggles I went through. Some cowered from the struggles while others rose above it and became leaders of the military brat pack.

That sense of belonging came to end in 1992 and 1993 when my father's job transferred us to Fort Worth, Texas, and I had to attend public school once again. My first year at Bryson Elementary School was an educational experience where racial slurs and derogatory remarks were used toward me as a means to support other students' own self-esteem and confidence. Bryson was the first school I can remember where the population was very diverse with culture and socioeconomic class. The school had Spanish speaking students, Laotian students, European students, Caucasian students, African American students, and, of course, a Korean student. Not one of these groups was safe from some type of harassment directly or indirectly. However, by this time, I had accepted myself as being different because of where I came from and how I looked. My hair was straight, I was a little bucked toothed, and when I smiled, you could barely see my eyes. However, my physical characteristics were used against me once more to strengthen others' self-esteem. During this time, I encountered some words you might be familiar with—slant-eye, string-head, chink, rice eater, chopsticks, and every once in a while, I would hear gook. At first, I did not understand why these words were used to characterize a person of color or different background, and to this day, I still do not understand. Is it bad to eat rice or to use chopsticks and have slanted eyes? These were the questions I pondered back when I was young, and sometimes, I ask my students the same questions when they try to make a derogatory remark.

If it were not bad enough trying to get used to a new school after moving from England, I was trying to get used to another school only three years later in El Paso, Texas. If it weren't hard enough trying to get along with a diverse population like Bryson Elementary, I was also trying to get along with high school kids who were 97 percent Spanish population. I was once again the minority. In fact, out of 1800 students at Burgess High School, only two were Asian. Talk about sticking out like a sore thumb! Being that it was so rare to see Asian students, I did not get stares or talked about but was embraced by the school. However, the racism and prejudice occurred on the sports field where I would hear "Chinatown" and "Chinese" from my opponents.

Adulthood

As I enter my next phase of life as an adult, I have experienced new ways to handle the issue of race. I have seen the world, traveled to many places, and encountered many different people. I have experienced racism within my own family, and race was an issue with my wife and her father before our marriage. I have two wonderful kids who are biracial, and I have parents who are Caucasian and Asian. The perspectives and ideas I have accumulated throughout the years from people and experiences and in the public and private school systems have offered a new grasp on life and the issue of race. I majored in history at Webster University not to teach the facts and dates, but to illustrate how detrimental people's actions, ideas, and words can be to society and individuals. In return, my wish is for my students to use that knowledge and educate the world about the issues of race and how we can live in a harmonious society. Now that I have two kids of my own and being part of a biracial marriage, race takes on a new meaning. Before marriage, the mindset of the single Korean male used race as a means to gain acceptance by embracing my ethnicity and educating my friends and others about my heritage; however, as time lingers on, will the same methodology work for my children in an age where the issues of race are a ticking time bomb?

Michael became a teacher to expose students to the challenges of our society and to support their finding ways to improve our world. What can you take from Michael's story as you think about your role as an educator?

_____

_____

_____

_____

The narratives contained in this chapter offer a myriad of opinions and experiences for us to contemplate as we continue our journey to learn about what challenges our multiracial students and what we can do as educators to support their personal and academic achievement.

Think about what you learned from reading these narratives. Write your responses to the stories below.

_____

_____

_____

_____

WHAT I LEARNED

- There is no such thing as different races.
- Race as a biological reality does not exist; racism does.
- There is no separate, multiracial species of people. Multiracial individuals are people who self-identify as such or are viewed by others as such because they possess a blending of the phenotypes that are stereotypically applied to different groups of people, artificially called *races* in the United States.
- People who identify as first generation biracial are using biological race as the basis for that definition—whether they understand this or not.
- Race was created to give economic advantage to its creators and provide a rationale for enslaving human beings.
- Color, hair, and other phenotypical genes do not bind together; therefore, within a single family, there is a variety of skin colors, hair textures, and other physical features. There is no fixed racial phenotype because there is no such thing as race.
- Culture is learned behaviors and race is often confused with culture.
- We often judge others based on cultural behaviors that we attribute to race.
- Race both *exists* and *does not exist* in the United States and throughout the Western world, and "racial issues are not about physical skin color but rather stem from the meaning and value people assign to skin color" (Singleton & Linton, 2006, p. 106).
- Present-day inequalities between so-called *racial* groups are not consequences of their biological inheritance but products of historical and contemporary social, economic, educational, and political circumstances (AAA, 1998).
- Learning the stories of others supports my growth in understanding the diversity of experience found in my educational setting.

What have you learned?

_____

_____

_____

_____

TAKING IT TO THE CLASSROOM: STRATEGIES TO BUILD COMMUNITY AND IMPROVE ACHIEVEMENT

- Create a safe environment.
- Build a community of learners who appreciate one another.
- Use humor to decrease stress and build community.
- Model your expectations for open dialogue.
- Invite people from different cultures to visit your classroom. When I taught a business writing class, I invited a business person each week to speak to the class, and I purposely chose persons from a variety of heritages and cultures.
- Help students develop the vocabulary they need to discuss difficult issues surrounding race and culture.
- Be patient. Students are beginning their lifelong journeys.

We examined the concept of race, and next, we continue our journey to examine what this means in the worlds of our students identified as biracial and multiracial. As Singleton and Linton (2006) state above, race both *"exists and does not exist"* in the United States and throughout the Western world and "racial issues are not about physical skin color but rather stem from the meaning and value people assign to skin color" (p. 106). This leads us to the question: *What are you?* We'll examine this question in Chapter 3.

SUGGESTED RESOURCES FOR ADDITIONAL READING ABOUT RACE

Bolgatz, J. (2005). *Talking race in the classroom.* New York, NY: Teachers College.

Delgado, R., & Stefancic, J., (Eds.). (1997). Critical race theory: An annotated bibliography. *Virginia Law Review*, 79, 461–516.

Landsman, J. (2001). *A white teacher talks about race.* Lanham, Maryland: Scarecrow Press.

Pollock, M. (2008). *Everyday antiracism.* NY: The New Press.

Root, M. (Ed.). (1992). *Racially mixed people in America.* Thousand Oaks, CA: Sage.

Spencer, R. (2006). *Challenging multiracial identity.* Boulder, CO: Lynne Rienner Publishers.

Wise, T. (2008). *White like me: Reflections on race from a privileged son.* Brooklyn, NY: Soft Scull Press.

Yosso, T. (2006). *Critical race counterstories along the chicana/chicano educational pipeline.* NY: Routledge.

Zack, N. (2002). *Philosophy of science and race.* NY: Routledge.

3

What Are You?

In Chapter 2, we examined race and found, according to the American Anthropological Association (1998), that there is no scientific basis for race. The narratives included in the chapter suggest there is no "one racial experience." Instead, each of us is a unique individual who perceives reality in a unique way. With that in mind, *what* are we? Let's continue our journey of *what we don't know we don't know* and examine this question.

What are you?

_____

_____

_____

_____

My answer would simply be a *White woman.* As a White woman, I have been asked, *"What are you?"* a few times, presumably because my skin, when tanned, makes me look *ethnic* and because my birth name is Bonita, which appears on my driver's license. In fact, when I travel, I receive comments from airport security when they see the name Bonita, which makes me feel they do not believe it is my real name. However, because I have parents who look *White* and the maiden name *Schnurbusch*, which sounds *White,* I never doubted I was White, and the question of *What are you?* hits me as amusing. It has never been a question that caused me to wonder about what I am. What about you?

Have you ever had to choose between your parents to identify yourself to others? If so, how did that feel?

_____

_____

_____

_____

When mixed identity individuals are asked, *"What are you?"* or *"Are you Black?"* their responses differ. Many interviewed agree these are among the most frequently asked questions they receive.

In the following paragraph, Maria Hernandez Oliver writes about her experience:

> *I clearly remember the first time I was made aware I was of a different race. I was four years old and playing on the preschool playground when a little girl asked me something I had not been asked before: "Are you Black?" I was dumbfounded, not because I was offended, but because I honestly didn't know the answer. When I asked my mom later if I was black, she had a good laugh and told me, "No, honey, you're Mexican."*

Diana Breckenridge says,

> *I've been asked, "What are you?" many times. Lots of times, the way I've responded is "Human" knowing they want something else.*

How do you think your students respond when they are asked, "What are you?"

_____

_____

_____

_____

IDENTITY LABELS AND DEFINITIONS

Think about your students' answers. Depending on where you teach, you may find that more and more students in your classrooms identify themselves in ways that are unfamiliar to you. A number of these students choose to identify as *mixed* or are identified as such by others. Others use different terms.

What is *mixed*? Mixed usually refers to people who are of two or more racial heritages. However, mixed identity is far more complex. The labels used for people who self-identify as mixed are many. The research supports the fact that in this country, we are all *mixed* to some degree (Jones & Smith, 2000, p. 3). Let that statement sink in. If we believe we are all mixed, it changes our perceptions of others.

Do you consider yourself mixed? Why, or why not?

_____

_____

_____

_____

Since the research supports that we are all *mixed* to some degree, the words *biracial, mixed,* and *multiracial* are challenged by some researchers as being inaccurate labels. Therefore, even though I use the term *multiracial,* I do not believe in the racial part of the term. Rainier Spencer (2006) challenges the use of this term in his book *Beyond Multiracial Identity,* and I agree with his argument. However, because the research about this topic refers to persons using this term, I too am using it in the book. Confusing? You bet.

For the sake of discussion, the terms in this book are used in the following way:

Biracial: a person born whose parents self-identify as two separate races, whether they profess a belief in biological race or not.

> *I have parents who are Caucasian and Asian.*
>
> —Michael Vaughn, Asian/White, Teacher

Multiracial: a person who self-identifies as having two or more separate racial heritages; it also includes biracial people.

> *My maternal grandmother was Irish and African American. My maternal grandfather was Blackfoot Native American and African American.*
>
> —Karen Hayes, African American/White/Blackfoot Native American, University Professor

Mixed: a person who self-identifies as having more than one racial heritage and/or parents of different races, whether defined biologically or socially.

> *The perfect category for me is mixed because I'm neither all black nor all white. I'm both.*
>
> —Chelsea Breckenridge, Mixed: African American/ White, Student

Monoracial: a person who self-identifies as the same racial category as both parents; I (Bonnie) would identify as monoracial—white.

WHAT IS THE DIFFERENCE BETWEEN MONORACIAL STUDENTS AND MULTIRACIAL STUDENTS?

Monoracial students belong to the same racial category as their parents. Multiracial students are children whose parents belong to two separate racial designations or categories. When we encounter people we assume are monoracial individuals, we fit them neatly into a box, however stereotypical. When we see someone who appears ambiguous to us because of their physical features, we find it more difficult to fit them neatly into a racial category.

What assumptions do you make about those who appear different than you?

_____

_____

_____

_____

PHENOTYPES

I make assumptions about those who appear different from me on the basis of their phenotypes. Phenotypes, as stated in Chapter 2, are the visible characteristics of an organism resulting from the interaction between its genetic makeup and the environment. They include one's physical features, and our phenotypes are usually what are used to place us into racial categories.

My phenotypes usually categorize me as white, but my first name Bonita cues others to question whether I'm Hispanic, considering I have olive skin and dark hair and eyes. Michael Tapp's phenotypes identify him as white, yet his brother's phenotypes identify his brother as black. Their parents are the same two individuals. Jacqui Felgate's phenotypes place her into categories of color, but she self-identifies as white, as do the rest of her Italian family.

In the following anecdote, Michael Tapp describes how his phenotypes caused others to misidentify him and the impact it had on his racial identity.

One (experience) that really sticks out also occurred in high school. I went to a party at a kid's house from another school with a group of my black friends. The entire crowd was black, which didn't bother me at all. In fact, I probably didn't even think about that fact. The kids from my school knew me, so I didn't worry about being given a hard time because of my skin color (or lack *thereof). There was music going, and people were dancing, so I decided to join in. All of a sudden I hear a kid near the DJ yell, "Look at that white boy dancing!" So everybody looked, and some of the kids from other schools laughed. I felt like I had a spotlight on me. I didn't understand why he wanted to point me out. I was doing the same dance as everyone else. I wasn't doing anything out of the ordinary. Then I looked back at the kid and saw the smug look on his face that said, "Know your place, white boy." I couldn't think of any reason he would want to call me out other than the fact that he thought I was trying to "be down" and he wanted to put me in my place. I remember not feeling "black enough" or as if I were inadequate. I was used to being an accepted member of the minority, and it felt very strange being made to feel as if I was anything but. That episode really made me question where I fit in. I thought I had earned my* pass *a long time ago. If I couldn't fit in with black folk, with the minority, where did I belong? Even though I look white, I'd never really looked at myself as a white boy until then.*

Michael's physical characteristics, or phenotypes, identified him as white to the teens at the party, yet Michael did not self-identify as a white boy.

Jacqui Felgate shares below how others judge her based on her phenotypes:

I attended college in a smaller southeastern Missouri town. I thought being in a college town and with the diverse population of students that filter in and out of the university that I would not run in to as many stares and questions. The first time that I realized that the stares and the questions would be a lifelong journey was when I met my first college boyfriend's parents. They were from an even smaller southeastern town (which sounds like I am making excuses). When it was time to meet the family, the questions and comments came up again. The first thing that was mentioned was "Black." I remember walking in the house (remember, I have never met these people before), and his younger sister came running up to me and said, "I saw you from the window, and you look Black, and my family does not like Black people!" I thought it was a joke. Who says those things? I looked to my boyfriend for help or an explanation, and all he had to say is, "Tell her what you told me." I was thinking, What did I tell you, you jerk?! So I then explained about being German, Irish, and Italian. She ran into the house to tell her mom that I was not Black but Italian. Then she asked her mom if that was okay and if that was any better than Black. I was devastated.

Jacqui's phenotypes, because they appear *ambiguous* to others, continually call her *racial categorization* into question.

In contrast to Michael and Jacqui, one mixed individual who was interviewed said she is never asked because her speech patterns, hair, and attitude *scream* Black. Her cultural markers, or phenotypes, identify her as Black.

Selena's description of her family illustrates how phenotypes appear in a variety of ways within a single family. In fact, individual genetic differences are no greater *between* persons of different races than they are *within* the same racial group.

Selena Shade Jimenez describes the impact of phenotypes in her family.

My mother, as I mentioned, is White. My father, whom I also mentioned, is Black and Cherokee Indian. There are five children in my family—my brother, my three sisters, and me. My brother is the oldest. He has olive-colored skin, and when he was younger, coarse, curly hair. He had two children with a white woman, and his children don't have Black features—they don't have to grease their scalps; they can wash their hair every day. My niece doesn't have Black features either, but she's only one year old. My oldest sister is married to a dark Black man. She has olive-colored skin. They have three children, and all three of them are light brown with visible Black features—coarse hair and gapped teeth. My nearest older sister is married to a Jamaican who has dark skin, but not as dark as my other brother-in-law. She also has olive-colored skin, and she has a gap in her front teeth, just like my younger sister and me. One of her sons has light brown skin, and the other has darker brown skin. They both have subtle Black features, and if they were just with their mother, you'd probably have to touch their hair to be really sure. I've told you about my family.... My younger sister isn't married and doesn't have kids. She has olive-colored skin and dark brownish black hair with natural blonde highlights just like my other two sisters. This is why I refer to my family as the Rainbow Coalition, and these are some of the features that make people ask us that RIDICULOUS question, "What are you?"

Selena describes her family as the Rainbow Coalition. Describe your family.

_____

_____

_____

_____

The examples above illustrate how *ridiculous,* to use Selena's word, it is to categorize others based on their phenotypes. Yet it is done. Again, if I am asked, "What are you?" my response would always be, "white woman." In fact, I wouldn't even say *white;* I'd just say *woman* because I don't usually have to think about race. As a white person, I am usually unmarked by race (although it impacts my life 100% of the time, according to Singleton and Linton, 2006, p. 76). I am just white, a member of the dominant group in the United States. I am not faced with questions about my ethnicity, nor do I have my behaviors challenged due to race. Race consciousness is seldom a topic of conversation unless I choose to initiate it. On the other hand, it is often different for those not possessing *white* phenotypes. Race consciousness just is. Maria Root (Root & Kelley, 2003), an expert on multiracial people, states in "Issues and Experiences of Racially Mixed People," that race consciousness is "brought up directly, sideways, and from all sides" for mixed individuals (p. 133, quoted in *Multiracial Child Resource Book*). The following statements illustrate this race consciousness in the lives of these two teachers.

> *Being biracial is a like being pulled in two different directions. You never feel as if you are on a solid middle ground. You always feel as if you are being pulled more towards one race than the other.*
>
> —Michael Tapp, Biracial, Teacher

> *I remember the shock that I felt when I found out that how I was different was a problem—a big problem for some. I did not feel acceptable, but I was not sure why.*
>
> Alicia Cooper (pseudonym), White/Black, Teacher

Describe your reaction to the above statements.

_____

_____

_____

_____

These teachers self-identify and relate their feelings regarding how that impacts others' perceptions of them as well as their own acceptance of themselves. As students in our classrooms confront their own race consciousness, so we, too, must strive to understand the complexities of their issues.

WHAT ARE YOU? AMERICANS ARE MULTIETHNIC

This all brings us back to: *What are you?* As you think about how you categorize yourself racially (if you do so), consider more deeply how that categorization impacts your life and the lives of those around you. If you are white, do you believe you receive privileges not available to persons of color? If you place yourself in a category other than white, how does that impact the ways in which you perceive the world? Finally, do we have conversations about these questions with our colleagues and our students?

Americans are multiethnic, and no matter how hard we try to maintain racial borders, personal lives prove the borders obsolete. Race was created to give economic advantage to its creators and provide a rationale for enslaving human beings, but in the 21st century, we must remove the shackles and release its hold on our country and our identities. In *Dreams*

From My Father, Barack Obama (1995) writes, "My identity might begin with the fact of my race, but it didn't, couldn't, end there. At least that's what I would choose to believe" (p. 111).

Discuss how you agree or disagree with President Obama's words.

_____

_____

_____

_____

What are you? is such a complex question in our racialized society. Hopefully, our journey to examine this question offers some answers and poses additional questions. The following narratives speak to the question of *what are you?* Please read them keeping in mind your own racial history, the information about race in Chapter 2, and the information about racial categorization in this chapter.

Edith Beard Brady attended the same prestigious K–12 prep school as Barack Obama. As you read her narrative, notice how educators misidentified her and imposed negative expectations based on cultural and racial stereotypes.

Edith Beard Brady, Scotch Irish/Japanese, Born 1954
Publisher, San Francisco
Transcribed telephone interview

My father is a native-born Caucasian American of Scotch-Irish descent, and he met my mother, who is Japanese, after World War II, in her native Japan. I am a first generation American. That differentiates me from many mixed kids today. I was born in Japan, but I am American by birth but born offshore. I came to the United States at the age of three and was raised bilingually until then. I can be in the DAR (Daughters of the American Revolution) because of my Dad's family that goes all the way back to Reverend Griswold on the Mayflower.

We lived in Hawaii, on the windward side of O'ahu, which was called "da country." We lived in the first subdivisions on that side of the island in a community defined by church and school. Mother wrote for the local Japanese language newspapers, translated scientific papers for the Department of Fish and Wildlife from Japanese into English, and played the organ for the local Episcopal Church. My dad was an engineer working for the Air Force. Of greater significance was that my dad was one of two White men on the street. I thought being White was what it meant to be different. I went to public school, and I spoke "Da kine" the Pidgin English, what the cane workers spoke, the indigenous language. I spoke it until second grade when we moved to San Bernardino, California.

I'm mixed, and most people in San Bernardino looked like my dad. I was the only kid in that elementary school who was mixed. There was one Jewish kid, one Mormon, and everyone else was Protestant or Catholic and White. In the '60s, religion was the big identifier.

In the '60s, I remember the way I spoke was funny, and I learned to speak Standard English very quickly. I was put in the slow reading group. I had previously been in the top tier, and I remember being really upset by that. I think it was because I spoke Da kine. I remember working really hard so I could move into the bluebirds. By end of second grade, I jumped track and was in the top group. I felt supported, included, and I did not feel singled out for being mixed. I liked school and started really excelling.

In 1963, we moved to Marin School District in Marin County, California, where I was put in with predominantly Catholic students, and I was the outsider because we were Protestant. My brother and I were the only two mixed-race kids in the school. We moved back to Hawaii when I was in fifth grade, and I returned to the same elementary school where I started kindergarten.

Now I was back with kids who looked like me, but due to my high test scores, I was sent to Punahou School (the school Barack Obama attended). It is the best school on the island—one of the best, one of oldest (founded in 1841), and one of the largest K–12 prep schools in the United States. I began sixth grade. Although Caucasian is the minority group in Hawaii, the school was 50% to 60% Caucasian with a few local students, military students, and Asians. (Today the racial mix is tilted heavily toward Asian Americans.) What's interesting about Hawaii is that everyone could tell what you were. They always think I'm part Hawaiian since I'm taller than someone of Japanese descent would be. I think I'm very clearly Hapa (someone of mixed Asian or Pacific Islander origin).

I knew my place. There were others like me. I was in an academic environment, enriched by wonderful teachers, not at top of the class but in the top 10% of the class.

My eighth-grade world was torn asunder when my dad yanked us out of Hawaii and moved us to San Antonio, Texas. That's the first time I encountered the ugly side of racism, the truly ugly side of racism. I was a big girl (5'6") in eighth grade with dark brown hair, brown almond eyes, and dark skin from sun. Dad dropped me off at the school to enroll. At Punahou, I'd skipped one year of math and was reading at the college level, but the administrators in Texas put me in all remedial classes because they thought I was Mexican.

What cultural and racial stereotypes did Edith contend with during her school years? Do you think this happens in schools today? If so, in what ways?

_____

_____

_____

_____

"Did you get algebra?" was my dad's first question when he picked me up from school. When he heard what happened, Dad moved me to a different

junior high where there were 15 kids in algebra. I was enrolled in all honors classes, got credit for high school algebra, and started in freshman geometry in high school. I was the only mixed kid in a school that was 70% white, 25% Mexican, and 5% black, with three Asians, two Chinese, and me.

At the same high school in San Antonio, I was placed in freshman honors English. The first day the teacher said, "This class is entirely too large. I will be giving drop slips tomorrow." The next day she gave a drop slip to each Hispanic student and to me. My big white father explained that they were not pulling me from honors English, and Mrs. F had to take me back. The kind of prejudice that exists in that culture still exists, but in the classroom, that was the only blatant display I encountered. I attended Vassar College. I didn't like Vassar, transferred to UCSB (the University of California, Santa Barbara), and I then attended the Publishing Procedures Course at Harvard University (a graduate school for publishing) and have enjoyed a long and distinguished career in publishing.

Being mixed was really important. My father always said, "You're not half and half—you're double." For him, it was the greatest genetic experiment in the world, choosing an Asian mother for his children—and my mother was brilliant.

My brother has two sons who see themselves as White. They tell me that, but their phenotypes are Japanese. My baggage is the movie The World of Suzy Wong. *Why is it that the Asian woman in a mixed love affair has to die? Why can it never be a happy ending? The message is that mixed race is bad, and if you're mixed race, you die. Look at* Madame Butterfly.

I have two friends who are a same-sex couple, one Jewish and one Japanese. They wanted me to check the Asian box on the forms, but I refused because then I have to deny half of who I am. At the same time, the Japanese woman's son is mixed race; what I feel I give to them is a model of what you are when you grow up. You blend in, you model. My cultural experience is to be in touch with what it means to be Japanese. I don't see it as negative.

Comment on Edith's final three sentences.

_____

_____

_____

_____

Edith says, "You blend in." Jacqui Felgate's experience has been just the opposite. She doesn't always blend in with her Italian family, and as a result, she has a particularly insightful cultural lens. Jacqui's story further illustrates the complications of racial categorization.

Jacqui Felgate, White, Born 1977
Special Education Teacher, St. Louis, Missouri
Written narrative

I was born in 1977 in Washington, DC, to a dad who is German and Irish and a mom who is Italian and German. I have dark hair and light eyes with olive skin that looks slightly tan in the winter and tans to the perfect color in the summer. We moved with my dad's job a lot when I was a baby. The first real memories I have are from 1982 when we moved to Missouri. We lived in a middle-class neighborhood that was 95% White and religiously diverse even though it was in walking distance to our Roman Catholic Church. I never remember a time when race was an issue in our house. I attended public school that was part of the desegregation program, and inclusion was just beginning. I felt that I was exposed to many types of people and situations.

In elementary school, I remember trying to fit in. I would tell the other kids that looked at me funny or would be brave enough to ask what I felt was the ever-present questions about my eyes and skin color that "my skin was just darker because when I was little my parents would take me to the beach, and after a while, my tan just didn't go away." Still to this day, friends that I have had since first grade remember that explanation. I have always felt a little different *than my friends. When meeting new people, the first comment was always, "You have such pretty eyes." I always knew that was my cue to explain that I was part German, Irish, and Italian.*

I attended college in a smaller southeastern Missouri town. I thought being a college town and with the diverse population of students that filter in and out of the University that I would not run into as many stares and questions. Later in life, when it came time to do tasks that required a check in the ethnic box, and I would check White, people would look at the check and wonder if I had made a mistake. Clearly, I did not look White-White, but you could see it in their expression that they would like to ask but just didn't know how—so I would get the ever present, "You have such pretty eyes" comment. (Some started to add, "Where did you get your eyes?" to the end of that statement.) I would then go into the ethnic make-up of my family, and again, when I said I was Italian, people, they would say, "Oh," and they go on about their business. One time, I went to renew my driver's license, and the lady wanted to know if I needed to change my race because it showed as White. I looked at her, put a fake smile on my face, and gave her the rundown about being part German, Irish, and Italian.

When my husband and I were thinking about having a baby, I went to the doctor for a check-up. She asked if my husband was Black or White. I said that he was White. She then went through a series of questions about family and personal history, and, after all of the questions (some of which of course led to exploring my ethnic background and my acknowledging that I was also White), she went on to say there could be some health issues for a baby from a mixed *couple having children, and she was glad that we didn't have to deal with those issues.*

Like mine, Jacqui's phenotypes often place her in racial categories that do not match her heritage. What did you learn about racial categorization from Jacqui's story?

_____

_____

_____

_____

Dennis Lubeck looks at life through a different lens—that of a Jewish male. I have learned so much from him over the years, and he continues to expand my understanding of how race evolved in this country.

Dennis Lubeck, White, Born 1942
Executive Director, International Education Consortium, St. Louis, Missouri
Written narrative

As an American Jew raised in the 1950s in a predominantly Jewish community and school, my friends and I thought of ourselves as white and different since we went to Hebrew and Jewish Sunday schools. Our school was 80% Jewish. We were so isolated that some joked that we thought Jewish holidays were national holidays. Still, we were assimilated and never thought of ourselves as a separate race in the United States. Different. Yes, but not racially different. We were taught to be grateful for the opportunities America offered Jews. I was not aware some Jews and non-Jews viewed Jews as a separate race in the late 19th and early 20th centuries, although my immigrant grandfather thought of Jews as a separate race and told me so when I married a non-Jewish woman. I knew, of course, that Jews were seen as a separate race in Germany and other parts of Europe. In the late 1950s, Jewish communities in the United States and elsewhere were anxious to move beyond the horrors of the Holocaust and return to the normalcy that American's civic culture offered. Holocaust studies and awareness as a centerpiece of Jewish identity was in the future and had little influence on us except that we heard from adults how anti-Semitic Germany and Russia were.

We were raised to believe that all people should have their basic rights but were not very cognizant of the racial divide or even the civil rights movement until we entered college in 1959. The Cold War seemed to be the dominant issue. Only further reading taught me that the pressures to create a positive U.S. image across the world inspired support for greater opportunities for blacks in the 1940s and 1950s.

This was the first time many of us found ourselves in a majority Christian environment. There were very few African Americans at the university. Jewish students avoided any total confrontation of what it meant to be a minority by joining Jewish fraternities. My younger brother entered the university in 1963 and roomed with the only black player at his level when the baseball team traveled for a road game. Jews were clearly seen as something different, even with their white skin.

Discuss what you think Dennis means in his last sentence when he says, "Jews were clearly seen as something different, even with their white skin."

_____

_____

_____

_____

I know we've done this before, but Dennis' piece reiterates the difference between culture and race. Reflect upon how you view the difference between the two—culture and race.

_____

_____

_____

_____

What most influences your identity: culture or racial categorization?

_____

_____

_____

_____

Val shares her life story and her educational experience in the following narrative.

Val Shumate, African American
Educator, Hospital School, North Carolina
Written narrative

As a veteran educator, I have fond memories of my family colors. During the early years (1950s) in coastal North Carolina, race and social races did make a difference. Despite racial differences and cultural struggles, we always managed to remain cordial and respectful toward whites and Indians. Rarely did we encounter interactions or associations with Asians or other immigrants.

Life was different in the armed forces for some of our relatives. They traveled to many foreign countries. My uncle met and married a German woman. My uncle's father was white, so he had distinguished Caucasian features. He returned to the States with his new family with great hopes of living the American dream. Our families shared happy memories together. Issues on cultural differences, tolerance, and acceptance were discussed openly most of the time.

The chapter continues as we fast forward to my work with multicultural students in 1977. I started my first teaching job in eastern North Carolina. The small town of James City is located between two major marine bases. They are Camp Lejune in Jacksonville, North Carolina, and Cherry Point in Havelock, North Carolina. The demographics are significant as there is an influx of racially mixed families that stay on these bases for two to six years. My work in the James City school was the beginning of family color dynamics, cultural differences, and the potpourri of relevant strategies for working with these children. My success with the multicultural children at a predominantly segregated school created a need for resource assistance in a neighboring school that had a 95% white student population.

I divided my week by serving each school for two and a half days. Behaviorally, the students experienced degrees of depression, conduct disorder, attention deficit disorder (ADD), attention deficit hyperactive disorder (ADHD) with defiance, oppositional behavior, and acting out. With effective parent/family therapeutic intervention, the multicultural students developed *and practiced social skills for dealing with diversity in the school and the community. The most memorable moments occurred after all of the drama when the students shared family cultural events in presentations.*

Val stresses the importance of her work with racially mixed students. Think about your work as you continue reading the narratives in the book.

Diana Breckenridge focuses more on racial categorization in her narrative and how that impacts her identity as she answers the question, *What are you?*

Diana Breckenridge, Black/White, Born 1978
Stan Breckenridge's Daughter, Optician, Los Angeles, California
Transcribed personal interview

A strong family background is the key to any successful child becoming an adult. It begins with two strong parents who are confident and who give a child what a child needs regardless of who they are or what they look like.

I came from a family that started off as a normal, typical family. When my parents divorced, that's when my brother and I started having problems.

I do not feel that I have a choice about race. There is no choice. There is no comfort you can get when you're mixed. If you choose to identify with one side or the other, you'll remember you're 50% the other thing, and people will remind you constantly that you are. You can do your best to identify with the one side or the other; however, you can never fit 100% into either side. Yes, I am in favor of mixed people being identified for exactly what they are, not just one or the other.

I think my physical markers that designate me to a particular race or classification are my hair texture and skin tone. It's so obvious to me. I do have finer features. However, even if someone has those characteristics, you could be completely wrong. I started opening up and really realizing I was different at about 13 years of age. I started understanding why I was being asked about my hair and other things that were different from the typical Caucasian children— all white area and all white school. As I got into junior high, that was the most difficult time of transition, turning into a teen and then knowing I was different and not wanting that kind of attention.

If we didn't have mixed people in the media, we might not have any positive attention at all. I do want to be identified as my own person, but if people want to identify me as Halle Berry, I'm complimented. Community demographics and economic status were important only in that they taught me who I wasn't—who I was not fully.

What issues does Diana raise regarding her mixed heritage?

_____

_____

_____

_____

Courtnee's answer to *What are you?* is complex. Her story encapsulates so many issues faced by students who find themselves identified by others in ways that often do not match their own feelings or self-identification.

Courtnee Cox, Black/Occaneechi Saponi (Occaneechi Band of the Saponi Nation)
Teacher, Chapel Hill, North Carolina
Written narrative

Growing up in a house with people who didn't have the same skin color as I never made me question anything until I went to visit my father's family. I don't remember how old I was, but it was after going to school. I asked my mother why she was white and my dad was brown. Her response was simple: "He's dark, and I'm light." Nothing else to it; that was the way I would live my life until second grade. Because my parents were divorced, I lived with my maternal grandparents. We didn't discuss race or color; people were just people. We went to church with light and dark people, light and dark people were relatives who came to visit, light and dark people would babysit the children in the family, and I had light and dark cousins around everyday. When I would visit my father's family, most of the people were dark, but that meant nothing to me. We were all family. From the way my cousins told me, "God made us all different colors in the crayon box, but we all were put in there together to be a family."

Second grade was a defining moment for me dealing with race. As always, I played with all different people—light and dark—and it never occurred to me that anything was different. We were standing around the classroom getting ready to dig into the magic container when my light friend told me that I couldn't play with them. I thought I had done something to hurt her feelings, so I asked. She told me that I hadn't hurt her feelings, but I couldn't play with them anymore because I was black. I can't recall if I said anything, but I do know that I turned away and did not tell anyone what was said to me. For me, I couldn't understand what she meant. I was brown. A light brown. What did it matter? We were all God's creations put into the crayon box to be family. I did understand that my friends were not my biological family, but from the way I grew up, we were still God's family. I never told anyone at home about my friend saying this to me. Instead, I did what I was taught. I was still kind to my friend and played with her when she let me. I also played with black people too. My mind kept telling me that some people were light and some were dark, but my heart led me to believe that it was more than that.

When I moved to a new school, my heart changed my mind. Most of the people at the new school were light brown and dark brown. In third grade, I was told by another light-brown girl, "You think you are better than anybody else just because you've got long hair. All you do is swing it around and around." She had no idea that she had just crushed my spirit! It took a long time for my momma to let me wear my hair down, and I was so happy. But from that point on, I wanted my hair in a ponytail. Having long hair made my black friends say I was "trying to be white." I didn't want to be white, but white looked like my family. I was in total confusion throughout the rest of elementary school, but I didn't ask my family. I just knew that someone was not telling me the truth. There was no crayon box. Some people were white, others were black, and they didn't get along. The only thing that saved me was going home and seeing that in my house, we did.

During middle and high school, I identified myself as black, but race was never a big deal. We talked about our rival high school being the rich, white school, but that was the extent of it for me. But during my senior year of high school, I faced challenges with scholarship applications. I felt discriminated against because of my race, but my counselors told me that they were only going by the scholarship guidelines. Mother spoke with the school, but she told me that I would still get scholarships without their help. And I did. College was truly a time of discovery, but also a time of confusion. At UNC (University of North Carolina), I was an active member of the Black Student Movement. I identified myself as a black, young woman. Going back to my family . . . race was not discussed. So on a visit home, I just asked my grandma, "Ola, what color are you?" She quickly said, "I don't have a color. I'm the color of water." This shocked me because I had just read a book with the same title. I wanted her to explain, so we sat down and talked. The story was mind blowing. Growing up, she lived in a poor neighborhood with blacks. Although her family didn't look like them, they were all poor, black people in their eyes. Throughout her childhood, she was just a light-skinned black girl who was struggling like everyone else to go to school and learn. She told me of times when people would tell her to get away from those "n—," but she was told to pay those ignorant folks no mind. But she went through some of the same thoughts I had growing up. She realized that something was different but never questioned it. She saw the difference when she got married and moved away to a different town.

Ola and Paw Paw saw themselves as light-skinned blacks but were treated differently by each community. During World War II, Paw Paw was told that he needed to step in line with the white soldiers, but he refused. From that moment, white soldiers with whom he'd been friends would not even look at him. When he returned from the war, he could not eat at one of his favorite restaurants. He was told to go to the back door to be served. He had identified with the blacks, so they would treat him that way. In the black community, he was accepted but always told, "Len, you know you got it made. You can pass when you want to and get everything you need." They sent their children to the neighborhood schools that were black. Again, they were just light-skinned black children at school with dark-skinned black children. When civil rights' fights took place, many whites couldn't understand why the Martin children were at a black school. As the years went on, everyone in the community just considered them the light-skinned black family.

Grandma Ola had never talked about her issues with race, but I saw that she didn't believe that she was black. It was just something that came to her—it was her label whether she liked it or not. Hearing this made me question myself. Am I wrong for claiming to be black? My father is black; my mother claims to be black, but is she? So many unanswered questions. Around 2000, our family got an answer to an unspoken question. My maternal family was not black. They were members of the Occaneechi Band of the Saponi Nation, a small Indian community in North Carolina. It had taken many painstaking years to discover this information. It finally gave my grandparents a real identity. The joy in my family circle was great. Although no one spoke about race before, I could tell that it was something everyone thought about. My aunts and uncle were busy learning about the tribe and having their birth certificates changed. Many of my cousins were doing the same, but I couldn't find the joy within myself. I couldn't give up being the black woman I had become. Changing my birth certificate meant that I had to give up my blackness. Black was beautiful to my family at one time, so I thought, but now it was changing. Family members were quick to say they weren't black, but they were Native Americans even when their fathers were black. This continues to be the case for me today. I have not attempted to change my identity, nor have I been extremely interested in becoming the Native I'm supposed to be according to some members of my family. I've been over this hundreds of times with my cousins, but I'm still considered to be crazy for not wanting to make that change.

In a recent conversation with coworkers, we were discussing the upcoming election. We were talking about our beliefs for education and how the candidates' beliefs fit with our own. As we talked, the conversation drifted to many other areas, and we saw that we all agreed in many areas. Our talk then went to the recent Yahoo poll that stated many white Democrats would not vote for Barack Obama because he is black. I said, "This is not news to me." But for a few of the teachers this was crazy. "Look how far we've come. Why does race matter?" Both questions were asked by white teachers who didn't believe the poll. These were some of the same teachers who were constantly unable "to do anything with those kids." "Their parents don't care, and I'm not spending my time if they don't do anything to help themselves," are statements that are made often at school. To me, these teachers were oblivious to their own actions to help perpetuate the view about blacks in America. As I reflected on our conversation, I realized that we needed to open up the conversation about institutionalized racism at school. When bringing this topic up at meetings . . . boy do I face some harsh criticism! Sometimes I do want to throw in the towel and do what I can, but I look at my younger cousins who are in elementary school right now. They have already shifted from being cute, little boys in kindergarten to behavior problems in third grade. When I am in the conversation with their teachers, I know that racism, stereotypes, cultures, and so on never come up in their teacher meetings. This is not acceptable, so I press on.

Comment on Courtnee's discussion of race. Do you find any of the challenges she faces to openly discuss race present in your school community? If so, how do you handle discussions about race?

_____

_____

_____

_____

The preceding narratives raise many questions. Write your questions below.

_____

_____

_____

_____

Once again, these narratives suggest that each of us lives a unique life, and even within the same culture and racial category, individuals are distinct and unique.

How has this chapter helped you answer the question, What are you?

_____

_____

_____

_____

WHAT I LEARNED

- Studying mixed-identity students gives educators the opportunities to learn more about *all* students not identified as white.
- Students not easily identified racially are often asked, "What are you?"
- Identity labels exist to categorize individuals.
- These identity labels depend upon phenotypes for categorization.
- I make assumptions about others based on their phenotypes.
- Making assumptions about others based on phenotypes is not scientifically based.
- Individuals vary as much within *racial groups* as they vary between *racial groups.*
- Issues of race weave their way through every aspect of our lives, including issues of identity that impact students in today's classrooms.

What have you learned?

_____

_____

_____

_____

TAKING IT TO THE CLASSROOM: STRATEGIES TO BUILD COMMUNITY AND IMPROVE ACHIEVEMENT

- Have students read stories from *What Are You?* listed in the Suggested Readings below. Use the stories to discuss point of view and cultural perspectives in English and history classes.
- Students can research how students learn math in different cultures. A colleague from Iran recently shared a method she learned as a

child to remember her multiplication tables. Sharing cultural strategies and stories builds bridges.

- When students do research papers, encourage them to tackle ethnic issues so they can learn more about each other's culture.
- Model disclosure. Depending upon the age level of your students, share your understandings about your own culture and ethnicity and encourage students to discuss theirs. These kinds of discussions can take place in the *final five minutes* of a class or week. This builds community and strengthens students' understanding of those who do not look like them. Note: students need to be taught how to talk about difficult issues and should have established *conditions* for the discussions. You can find discussion conditions in *Courageous Conversation About Race* and in *How to Teach Students Who Don't Look Like You.*
- Encourage interethnic cooperation as well as cooperation between ethnic groups of students.
- Students draw themselves and use their drawings to create a collage on a classroom wall.
- Each day one student introduces himself or herself over the public address system and shares cultural facts.

Consider having conversations about the assumptions listed above. When we address and include biracial and multiracial people in the context of our conversations, we change the conversation. No longer can we count on a static picture of race, one with firm boundaries of Black or White or Yellow or Red. Mixed and Multiracial people put race in the face of all of us.

This chapter includes definitions of mixed identity. In addition, you were asked to think about who you are and how you identify yourself. Our journey continues in the next chapter as we examine the challenges, myths, and stereotypes that mixed-identity students face in their lives.

SUGGESTED READING

Gaskins, P. (1999). *What are you?: Voices of mixed-race young people.* NY: Henry Holt and Company.

Obama, B. (1995). *Dreams from my father: A story of race and inheritance.* NY: Three Rivers Press.

O'Hearn, C. (1998). *Half and half: Writers on growing up biracial and bicultural.* NY: Pantheon Books.

Root, M., & Kelley, M. (Eds.). (2003). *Multiracial child resource book: Living complex identities.* Seattle, WA: Mavin Foundation.

4

What Are the Challenges for Multiracial Students?

I f, like me, you believe mixed-identity students may face experiences you *don't know you don't know,* then our journey continues with a discussion of these challenges. In this chapter, students and educators, children and parents—persons who identify as monoracial and multiracial—share their experiences so that we can better understand how race impacts all of our lives.

WHAT CHALLENGES DO MULTIRACIAL STUDENTS FACE?

Stan Breckenridge, an African American professor of musicology on the West Coast, and Graig Meyer, an educator in a North Carolina school district on the East Coast, share a common concern about their adolescent daughters. They each worry about the way their daughters will be treated by their peers. I too worry about my son. Not an uncommon worry for any parent, but our worries differ in that we worry that our biracial daughters and sons will be shunned by the white kids for being too black and shunned by the black kids for being too white. What is this all about, and as an educator, do you understand these fears?

How many students in your school fall between the races? What do you know about them?

_____

_____

_____

_____

How do we handle our fears? Stan and Graig share how they hold courageous conversations about race with their daughters, for keeping silent about race communicates that race is a nonexistent or illegitimate topic for conversation (Rockquemore & Laszloffy, 2005, p. 97).

On the other hand, I was often afraid to talk about race with my son. Instead, I took him to every cultural event I could afford, but seldom did I ever talk with him about how he felt about being different. I have concern about what I didn't do as the mother of a biracial son, and I now believe that parents cannot afford to be silent. Teachers too cannot afford to be silent.

How have you dealt with issues of race and multiraciality in your schools?

_____

_____

_____

_____

If we say we "don't see color" and refuse to confront issues of race openly, honestly, and respectfully, we may communicate to our students of color that we are dismissive of their personal experiences. Students want to share their experiences.

What specific challenges might multiracial students face?

_____

_____

_____

_____

Are these challenges different for multiracial students than for other students of color? If so, name them.

_____

_____

_____

_____

Why is it important for you to know the challenges that multiracial students face?

_____

_____

_____

_____

MULTIRACIAL GROUP IDENTITY

People of mixed descent have always been a part of this country. So if this is true, when, why, and how did multiracial people become a self-identified group?

When

Before the 1960s, racial classification was usually thought of as something government imposed. What changed in the latter part of the 20th century were the multiracial activists who argued "ethnoracial self-identification was a person's right" (Winters & DeBose, 2003, p. 69). This is a relatively recent phenomenon.

Why

Multiracial activists began the movement to self-identify as a separate group in the last decade of the 20th century because they felt it was their right.

How

Are there more *mixed* people now? There *are* more mixed people now because there are more people, and children of the *biracial baby boom* of the 1960s are now seeking to have their identities recognized. Between 1960 and 1990, intermarried couples increased from about 150,000 to 1.5 million with children increasing from 500,000 to two million (DaCosta, 2007, p. 7).

However, growth in numbers does not explain the organizational growth that took place among mixed people. Since "there is no group *history* or culture that all mixed-race people share, participants in multiracial organizations and expressions of multiracial identity coalesce around a notion of *mixedness* rather than racial sameness" (p. 7).

What does it mean that there is "no group history" that all mixed race people share?

_____

_____

_____

_____

Unlike ethnic cultures that share common histories, ethnicities, or heritages, these different groups of mixed-identity individuals do not share these commonalities. Instead, they bond together around their mixedness to be advocates for multiracial categories on the U.S. Census and other forms.

MULTIRACIAL ADVOCACY GROUPS AND CENSUS 2000

Multiracial advocacy groups began to form in the late 1970s and continue today. Groups sometimes disagreed, and early alliances were broken as groups struggled to find an acceptable compromise for the 2000 Census. Advocacy groups wanted a separate box for multiracial individuals. Other groups fought this, stating that a separate box would dilute the political power of others in separate categories that were nonwhite. The result was the *check-one-or-more-box* format used in the 2000 Census.

The check-one-or-more-box format on the 2000 Census was the result of this advocacy in cooperation with other civil rights organizations and ethnic special interest groups. This box accomplished three things: it allowed for the "celebration of diverse heritages"; it supported the "continued monitoring of existing civil rights legislation that impacted multiracial people directly"; and it provided the "most information for the accurate collection of racial/ethnic data for medical diagnosis and research" (Root & Kelley, 2003, p. 15). This was seen by many as a step forward.

Yet despite working together, there is a concern from some civil rights groups and laypeople that the multiracial movement is working to achieve a higher *whiter* racial status for multiracial people than exists for monoracially identified Blacks, Asians, and Hispanics. Some groups believe the higher whiter racial status is a desire for white privilege that leaves other people of color behind. However it is perceived, several groups continue to advocate for multiracial people, holding conferences, working on transracial adoption issues, and assisting government agencies with compliance issues.

You can find information about advocate groups and additional resources in the *Multiracial Child Resource Book: Living Complex Identities* (2003). Maria Root coedits this book published by the Mavin Foundation. A nonprofit organization, the Mavin Foundation states its mission as "redefining diversity through innovative projects celebrating multiracial and transracially adopted youth and families" (Root & Kelley, 2003, copyright page). This comprehensive resource guide gives statistical information about multiracials; extensive authored chapters on identity and development of multiracials; authored chapters on specific multiracial heritages; and resources, including books, films, Web sites, and references.

Why Are Multiracial Students Who Don't Have White Skin Usually Placed in the Nonwhite Racial Designation?

The answer to this question is complex with historical roots. It is because of hypodescent, or the *one-drop rule*. The one-drop rule legally ensured that biracial people of African American descent be identified as black. This social system assigns a mixed individual to the racial group in their heritage that has the *lowest* social status. For example, one drop of black blood makes a person black. This was begun in the 1600s to keep mixed-race people in slavery. Today, 30 million African Americans in this country are already mixed, and claiming Blacks to be monoracial is historically false. This is a huge shift in thinking for me. I always thought African Americans were Black people, but after learning more about race—or should I say the absence of its scientific reality—I must shift my thinking to see that all people of color, and for that matter all *White* people in this country, are to some degree mixed. Yet for those who visibly have enough melanin in their skin and whose phenotypes conform to our stereotypical ideas of particular categories, hypodescent, or the one-drop rule, continues to impact their status in different ways than it impacts mine.

Reflect on this part of our nation's history.

_____

_____

_____

_____

Hypodescent, the one-drop rule, continues today in social as well as political contexts. Some believe if a biracial person of African American and European American descent selects any designation other than

African American, they do not want to embrace a dual heritage and want to remove themselves from a perceived inferior race in order to receive white privilege (Winters & DeBose, 2003, p. 129). White privilege refers to "the advantages that White people receive simply by virtue of their appearance and, to a lesser degree, the privilege lighter-skinned people of color garner as compared to darker members of the same or different non-white racial groups" (Singleton & Linton, 2006, p. 183). If one believes white skin color brings with it privilege, those who possess it could possibly remove themselves from the negative effects of being black in our society while benefiting from the positive effects of being white. Those who dispute white privilege could point to the election of Barack Obama, the first person of color elected to be President of the United States.

Obama (1995) discusses the impact of hypodescent upon his life in his memoir, *Dreams From My Father*. While discussing issues of his mixed heritage, Obama writes his multiethnic friends "talked about the richness of their multicultural heritage, and it sounded real good, until you noticed that they avoided black people. It wasn't a matter of conscious choice, necessarily, just a matter of gravitational pull, the way integration always worked, a one-way street" (pp. 99–100). With the friends he describes, the gravitational pull seems to be towards privilege. Obama stresses his individualism, which he perceives goes beyond the phenotypical categorization that others use to place him into racial categories. The fight for and the right to be an individual is deeply ingrained in this nation's psyche, yet definitions of race segregate people into categories that cause them to be judged first by their skin color rather than by the content of their characters. Phenotypes often take precedence over personality, individualism, and character. Do you believe the election of Barack Obama will change what he describes above?

Reflect upon what you read above.

_____

_____

_____

_____

The one-drop rule weaves its way throughout our society in areas of allocation of resources and psychological ramifications. It no longer keeps individuals physically enslaved, but it still exerts influence over people's choices and opportunities. My son, who is usually viewed by others as being African American, interviewed for a job working in a Latino area. The interviewer told him that his darker skin color gave him an advantage for the position. My son was glad to have the advantage. This time his darker skin color had value, and he got the job. As Singleton and Linton

(2006) state in *Courageous Conversations About Race*, "racial issues are not about physical skin color but rather stem from the meaning and value people assign to skin color" (p. 106). We will examine skin color more closely in a later chapter.

What about the lives of your students? In what ways is their skin color valued or not valued?

_____

_____

_____

_____

Most of the issues multiracial students face are the same issues all students of color confront since they consist of lowered expectations and discriminatory practices. However, there are some experiences that are different for multiracial students, and this chapter examines these.

MIXED-IDENTITY STUDENTS FACE MYTHS AND STEREOTYPES

Mixed-identity students face myths and stereotypes. What myths and stereotypes have you encountered regarding multiracial students?

_____

_____

_____

_____

One challenge multiracial students face is the legacy of myths and stereotypes that have been assigned to them throughout history. Fortunately, most former pathologies assigned to multiracial students are now regarded as myths. Since it was never my assumption as the mother of healthy, happy multiracial children, I was surprised to find in the early research (most before the 1990s) that students of mixed race were thought to be pathological.

Diana Breckenridge, the daughter of Stan Breckenridge, whose narrative is found in an earlier chapter, describes her feelings:

Monoracial people think there is a problem with us, but there is no problem until we start getting treated badly by monoracial people who don't understand us. There isn't a discrepancy within biracial people; there is a problem with monoracial people who don't understand.

Current research supports Diana Breckenridge's assertion "that there is nothing inherently wrong" with biracial people. Yet myths and stereotypes have prevailed throughout the 20th century about the pathology of mixed, biracial, and multiracial children and adults. In a 1920 essay for *Good Housekeeping,* Vice President Calvin Coolidge wrote that laws were necessary to separate whites from others because the "hybrid is clearly both a diseased entity that could only perpetuate that illness and a sign of a monstrous union of different races" (Squires, 2007, p. 32)**.** For this to be written by a Vice President and published in such a mainstream magazine illustrates how widely accepted were these myths.

As late as 1944, scientists still published work on the degeneracy of "mixed bloods" filled with theories of the maladjusted or "marginal" man (p. 33). The mixed-blood person was "theorized in social science as a problem and one to be avoided by retaining existing social and legal restrictions on race mixing" (p. 33). The media often portrayed interracial families in ways that exploited fear and stereotypes with the "tragic, mulatto-raised-by-single-white-mother" story used as a "subtle cautionary tale" against interracial relationships (DaCosta, p. 123). In Hollywood films, the mixed person's story often ends unhappily.

Donna Rogers Beard, whose racial narrative appears in Chapter 2, cites the influence of media stereotypes upon her journey to understand race:

> *[In college] I continued to think about the issue of miscegenation. The pop culture message of the tragic mulatto had intrigued me since I discovered the historical novels of Frank Yerby when I was about twelve years old. His antebellum southern fiction focused on miscegenation. The results were often tragic. Earlier, I had been exposed to* Pinky, *one of the first Hollywood films about race mixing. It is the story of a young woman in the north, passing for white, who has to choose between her black grandmother and her white boyfriend who is a doctor. In 1959, Hollywood remade* Imitation of Life. *This ultimate tragic mulatto film was first released in 1934, and the lead role was played by Fredi Washington, a woman of color. Washington became a real life tragic mulatto because Hollywood did not know what to do with a black woman who was light enough to pass for white. When the movie was remade in 1959, the same role was played by a white Susan Kohner. Twenty-five years later, the message was still the same: black people who were racially ambiguous were destined to a tragic life. The only way to escape this destiny was to choose to be black. This genre of film was a minor part of the box office offerings of the late '40s, the '50s, and into the '60s, but played a prominent role in my life.*

Recent research does not support the destiny of a tragic life for mixed identity individuals. In fact, there is no definitive research that states mixed students live a more complex life, but they do lead a different life experience. The onset of the 21st century finds multiracial students at a transitional moment in history, and this is all the more reason why we need to be aware of the possible challenges they may confront. Yet you may find no difference between your mixed students and other students. Your mixed students may be fully integrated socially and may experience no more challenges than any other students of color. On the other hand, your mixed-identity students may be experiencing challenges that manifest themselves in your school setting, and therefore, it is important that you are aware of these. In Chapter 6, we meet Kim Anderson, a therapist who specializes in working with multiracial students, and she shares her expertise about the challenges these students face. One such challenge is the racial identity development of mixed children, which is explored in Chapter 6.

Since much of the pathological literature about mixed-identity children was written by psychologists and sociologists about children who were referred to them, it was only natural that the children would be described as misfits, since that was the reason they were being studied by these professionals in the first place.

Thanks to a wider breadth of research in the 1990s and beyond, we now know that mixed children, when raised in a psychologically sound family, develop as psychologically sound as any other children. I found it interesting that a *label* or myth could be attached to an entire group of people based on the few who were referred for misbehavior or mental disorder. Learning that helped me understand how stereotyping operates.

As an educator, I want to know the stereotypes assigned to students of mixed race. In *School Counselors' Perceptions of Biracial Children: A Pilot Study*, Henry L. Harris (2006) cites the following stereotypes about biracial children:

- They are misfits with identity issues.
- They will experience possible rejection by all ethnic groups with inclusion in none.
- They will have trouble determining their role in society.
- They will face enormous guilt if they culturally identify with one parent and reject the other.
- They do not want to talk about their racial heritage.
- They must identify with the parent of color since they will be judged to belong to that group. (p. 2)

Do any of the above stereotypes fit your current thinking? If not, how might you combat the stereotypes?

_____

_____

_____

_____

Additionally, Francis Wardle (1992), in *Supporting the Biracial Children in the School Setting* states additional myths about interracial families and biracial children:

- People who marry into other racial or ethnic groups are perverted.
- Minorities accept biracial children better than nonminorities.
- Interracial marriages more often end in divorce.
- The fact that the child is biracial is a far greater difference than any other individual difference such as disabilities, gender, and giftedness, suggesting that this difference will have a greater negative impact than what other children experience. (pp. 2–3)

Wardle states that teachers must examine their feelings about biracial children, and if they believe the myths about these children, they should not work with them. Perhaps a better solution might be professional development for teachers to dispel the myths and build a knowledge base for the teachers about mixed students.

While it is true that a multiracial student may experience any of the above, these stereotypes do not describe the experiences of all multiracial students. If school counselors and teachers hold any of these negative stereotypes about multiracial students, it places an unfair burden on students to prove the stereotypes wrong (just as negative stereotypes placed upon all students of color places the burden of proof on the child).

How do you deal with the myths and stereotypes surrounding your students of color?

_____

_____

_____

_____

We must find ways to break down the myths and stereotypes that surround our students. One way to do this is to look for strengths in our students.

A word of caution: When we read these studies, we need to read critically and not automatically assign certain behaviors to multiracial students, for if we do, we merely reinforce stereotypes rather than use the information to broaden our understanding of challenges that *may* occur in the lives of our mixed identity students.

The following two narratives outline challenges, myths, and stereotypes Michael Tapp and Tahnee Markussen have faced. They were born during the same decade, live in the same city, and both self-identify as being biracial children of one black parent and one white parent. They were born after the Civil Rights Movement, and they are beyond adolescence and well into adulthood.

Michael Tapp, Biracial, Born 1974
Teacher/Elementary School, Omaha, Nebraska
Written narrative

Experiences of a Biracial Individual in America

Childhood

My first recollection of being biracial occurred when I was seven. We were living in Texas at the time. My dad got a job as a football and basketball coach down there. I vividly remember sitting in the crowd at a basketball game next to another kid about my age. I pointed out my dad, who was coaching at the time, to him. The kid asked me straight-faced, will no ill intent, if I was adopted. It took me aback because I had never had any thought of being anybody's but my mother and father's. That was the first time that I can recall being different *and really realizing that I was biracial and that other people saw me as something other than just another seven-year-old kid. From that point on, I became conscious of my race.*

Adolescence

My biracial identity really matured during my adolescence. Many people consider adolescence a time when you begin to form a personal identity, and that held true for me. Although much of my familial interaction had been with both black and white people, the majority of my friends up until that point had been white. That changed during junior high. I went to an inner-city junior high school. I was surrounded by "my people"—black people, white people, Hispanic people, Asian people, and more importantly to me, biracial people. My best friend in junior high and through high school was also biracial, but we were biracial opposites: my father was black, his was white; my mother was white, his was black; I looked white, he looked black; I was treated as being white, he was treated as being black. Having another person outside of my family who was also biracial and could relate to many of the things I could was great for me. But it was also the general feeling that permeated the school. People of various races could hang out with each other without receiving sideways glances or comments. I can recall a slumber party we had at my friend's house during eighth grade. There were six of us there: two biracial kids, one Native American kid, one Greek kid, one black kid, and one white kid. It was a slumber party the United Nations would have been proud of. I was in my element, and I think it was at this time that I really discovered that I was most comfortable in a very diverse setting rather than in a setting that primarily consisted of one race or another.

I also went to an inner-city high school. I had many of the same friends and had similar experiences as that of junior high. However, at this time I started to branch out into the world thanks to my friends' and my drivers' licenses. It was then that I discovered that I was in a pretty protective bubble and that many people outside of that bubble didn't appreciate diversity in the same way I did. With age, I was also becoming more conscious of my race and how other people viewed me based on my race.

The first experience that really heightened my awareness of my minority status occurred when I was sixteen. I was dating a young lady who was white. One day, she went to introduce me to her grandmother. We went over to her house, and she was very grandmotherly. She gave us both a hug, served us some cookies, and was very pleasant. I thought she was a very sweet lady. Days later, I asked my girlfriend if we could go over to her grandmother's again. She said we couldn't because she had told her grandmother that I was half-black, and her grandmother had told her that I was not welcome there anymore. I had always known that I was a minority, but that was the first time I can remember being discriminated against because of my race, and it hurt.

College

College was my next big life experience. I decided to go to a small, private college because they had a good academic reputation and because they would allow me to play two sports. I honestly didn't know what to expect. But if you think my protective bubble burst before, it was about to explode in college. The school I went to was a majority of white, small-town kids. I could count the number of minority students on my hands (if you counted the students from other countries in study abroad programs, then I would have to use my feet.) I was completely out of my comfort zone, but since it was college, I figured it was a good chance to learn. And boy, did I learn some things.

My first roommate was a friend of mine from high school who happened to be black. Our next door neighbors consisted of one black kid and a white kid who also went to an inner-city high school. These were the people I hung out with the most. We ate together, went to parties together, and just kicked it a lot. That was normal to me, but for many of the other students at the school, it was not. In the cafeteria, there was one table where we normally sat—the black table. This was where the minority kids would sit. I sat there because that was where my friends sat, and honestly, it was where I felt most comfortable. But not everyone was comfortable with me being there. I could tell it made them uncomfortable from the glances over to our table. I felt they didn't understand me. The way I dressed, the way I talked, and the way I carried myself told them that I was trying to be black and not trying to be myself. Many of them had never had a friend of another race, and they felt that doing so meant that you were trying to be like them.

Because I looked white, they felt safe telling these jokes. But inside, I felt as if I were a spy. I was the black man with a white disguise who could point out who the real racists were. At the times when my cover was blown and they found out or remembered I was half-black, the usual comment was, "I didn't know. I'm sorry."

Adulthood

After college, I eventually settled back in my hometown and currently teach fourth grade. Most of the experiences that molded me as a biracial individual took place during my adolescence and college years. Adulthood has consisted more of becoming comfortable with who I am as a person, not just a biracial person. The incidences regarding my race have decreased, if not almost disappeared. There are still times that I become cognizant of my race. At those times, I feel a bit uneasy explaining that despite the fact that I look white, I am in fact biracial. However, many of the strange looks and awkward comments have lessened quite a bit.

Because our country tends to want to put people into convenient categories, and biracial individuals don't have a recognized category, we continue to be other. *My hope is that one day we will have our own categories, so that children don't have to continue to feel like a second-class citizen as I did whenever I had to color in the* other *circle.*

I wish that I were able to openly talk about my racial background as a kid. I wish I would have had a forum to discuss my experiences and have a little back-and-forth with my peers. I would also have liked to learn more about them too and where they came from. I feel that such open discussion can help people of various races, religions, sexual orientation, and so on. I relate it to the story of my maternal grandparents. They weren't accepting of my father simply because he was black, but once they got to know him as a person, they came to love and appreciate him as a person. I think that if we get to know people for who they are and not what they are, we can make huge strides in race relations, and kids won't have to go through some of the things I had to go through as a kid.

Tahnee Markussen, Biracial, Born 1973
Education Director, Omaha, Nebraska
Written narrative

I am a biracial, 35-year-old native Nebraskan. I was adopted by white parents from small towns. My two older brothers are white, and my younger sister is also biracial and adopted. I have met my biological mother. She has three other kids younger than I (all white). She had me when she was 15 years old and was forced to give birth to me miles away at a group home. Afterwards, she had to give me up for adoption or go into foster care where they would have taken me from her anyway. My father's parents wanted to keep me, but her parents didn't want me in the same small town. My father was also 15 years old.

I didn't know I was different until I went to an elementary school event at my brother's school. Someone said, "Look at the little black girl" (I had an afro back then, and it was much easier to determine my race), and I looked around the room for someone that looked like the color of coal. My mother realized what I was doing and said, "They are talking about you." I busted out crying. She didn't realize that I had no idea I wasn't white with blond hair like my older brothers.

My racial awareness increased when we moved from Kearney, Nebraska to Lincoln, Nebraska. There were more blacks in Lincoln Junior High, and that heightened my racial awareness. I thought I should fit in with the black girls since the white girls didn't want to be friends with me. But the black girls always made fun of me and would try making me fight with the other biracial girl in my grade. Junior high sucked. I began to think that in order to be who I thought I was supposed to be, that is black, that I had to be mean and pushy. And unfortunately, I developed into that kind of person for a very long time. Now, I identify as a black woman. Not what I thought a black woman was growing up. I am my own black woman. I used to have an exaggerated emphasis on my appearance. I used to hate my hair. Hate the color of my skin after it tanned, hate my butt.

My adopted mother found my biological father when I was in my early 20s. I love my dad's side of the family—only 'cause they are so very intriguing, and they act as if I've always been around. My grandparents are Baptist (my grandpa was a Baptist preacher before he passed away); my Uncle Jack is a Mormon (Black Mormons? Who would have thought?); my

Aunt Tina (my dad's sister) is a Catholic; and her daughter, my first cousin Saundra, converted to Judaism over ten years ago. I am a practicing Buddhist, which isn't too popular with black Christians, but come on; it makes more sense than black Mormons.

My father has a good life in Bethlehem, Pennsylvania. He has been working in professional motor sports since he was a teenager. He's one of very few black men in the profession. My biological mother has been fighting a drug addition. I haven't talked to her since early 2000; I hope she is doing all right.

Growing up, I had a very hard time fitting in anywhere. I hated myself for a long time, and only recently within the last ten years, I have found comfort in my own skin. I cannot tell you how good it feels to finally be at home. I have a degree in journalism from Creighton University. I have three children: an eight-year-old boy and twin, three-year-old girls.

We have no choice *to choose which group to belong to—we are damned if we do and damned if we don't make a choice. People think I'm Hispanic, Asian, Indian, Eastern Indian . . . . People think I am everything I am not. When I was younger, pejorative language whittled away at any semblance of who I thought I was. I now assert my mixed-race identity by being myself. Enjoying things from all cultures and embracing things, I no longer do things because society says I should, as a "black woman," do this or not do that. I hate hearing black people say things such as, "That's white people stuff," because that implies that they are excluding themselves from an experience based on their skin color. They are, in effect, cutting themselves off from things that might make them happy.*

These days I could care less what people think of my hair; some days it is straight, some days curly. When I was growing up, I despised my natural look. I have pretty ambiguous features though, so they were never a problem. Community demographics and economic status influenced my group identification. My Medicaid glasses surely defined my social class, making my maneuvering in life much harder than it should have been. Upper-class, biracial people are more inclined to the benefits of white privilege *than poor, biracial people, even though all biracial people never get to fully experience all of the privileges white people of any economic status enjoy.*

Michael's and Tahnee's narratives share common ethnic heritages. What challenges do you find in their narratives?

_____

_____

_____

_____

What myths and stereotypes do you find in their narratives?

_____

_____

_____

_____

What did you learn from reading Michael's and Tahnee's narratives?

We have now read several narratives from individuals who deal with mixed identity. As educators, we hunger for strategies to support the students with mixed identity who populate our classrooms.

Many strategies that are useful are the same strategies we find in powerful books on instruction. However, students may also benefit from the following.

WHAT I LEARNED

- Multiracial students encounter different experiences from white students.
- Multiracial students encounter similar experiences that face all students of color.
- Multiracial students may encounter unique experiences that differ from both white students and other students of color.
- Keeping silent about issues of race communicates that these issues are nonexistent or illegitimate topics for conversation.
- Myths and stereotypes about mixed people persist in the literature and media.
- Mixed children, when raised in a psychologically sound family, develop as psychologically sound as any other children.
- Interracial families possess strengths as well as face challenges in society.

What have you learned?

TAKING IT TO THE CLASSROOM: STRATEGIES TO BUILD COMMUNITY AND IMPROVE INSTRUCTION

- Embed cultural references within your lessons. Does this take more time on your part? Of course it does, but the benefits are huge.

Students respond to personalized lessons, and when they *hear and see* themselves in your lessons, it tells them you care enough about them to learn about other cultures and incorporate culturally proficient strategies into your instruction.

- Add a cultural fact to the morning announcements. Yes, this is fairly superficial, but if done well, it can help create a school climate where students expect to hear about all kinds of students and cultures.
- Post words on the walls from the languages your students speak. Use the words. Few things make a child so welcome as hearing his native language. We teachers can learn a few words, if not more, of the languages our students speak if we truly want to touch their hearts and minds.
- When students write research papers, encourage them to tackle ethnic issues so they can learn more about their own culture and others' cultures.
- Once again, incorporate a writers' workshop model that encourages students to share their feelings and use inquiry as a tool for learning.

What successful strategies have you tried?

_____

_____

_____

_____

At this point in the journey, I realize that there are issues about which I had been previously unaware. Becoming aware of these issues better equips us to face situations that may arise in our schools and supports our understanding of the journeys our multiracial students take as they navigate their way to identifying themselves.

This chapter continues to build background knowledge about multiracial students as well as offer educational strategies we can use to improve instruction for our students. We now continue our journey and dig more deeply into the topic of racial identity development and its impact upon our students.

SUGGESTED RESOURCES

Chito Childs, E. (2005). *Navigating interracial borders: Black-white couples and their social worlds*. Piscataway, NJ: Rutgers University Press.

Root, M. (Ed.). (1992). *Racially mixed people in America*. Thousand Oaks, CA: Sage.

Yosso, T. J. (2006). *Critical race counterstories along the chicana/chicano educational pipeline*. NY: Routledge.

5

How Mixed-Identity Students Develop Racial Identities

Do mixed-identity students develop their identities in ways that differ from other students in our classrooms? The research, for the most part, suggests they do. If they do, what do we need to know about the racial-identity development of these students? Our journey now takes us to the research on racial-identity development and narratives that speak to the process of identity.

In *Raising Biracial Children,* Rockquemore and Laszloffy (2005) state that "multiracial children growing up today exist at a transitional moment in history—when race is both real and unreal, trapped somewhere between the enduring legacy of slavery and the promise of the Multiracial movement" (pp. 159–160). The 21st century finds multiracial students at a transitional moment in history, and this is all the more reason why we need to be aware of the challenges they face. One such challenge is the process of racial-identity development.

What thoughts come to mind when you hear the term racial-identity development?

_____

_____

_____

_____

One thought that comes to my mind is how the word *other* is used to describe individuals who don't clearly identify as belonging to one racial group. What does *other* mean to the individuals who share their narratives?

Selena Shade Jiménez shares how she feels about the word *Other* as a designator of her racial identity.

> *I reminisce on the time when my two older sisters, another biracial brother and sister, and I all met outside one day after school at the end of my freshman year of high school in 1996. We were all very excited, and, without communicating with each other, we all knew why—we had FINALLY gotten a "Biracial" box on the California Achievement Test! (This test is similar to the End-of-Grade tests North Carolina students must now take.) We couldn't believe it. I was the youngest of the group—my younger sister was in the third grade, so she wasn't in the same school, and my brother was already out of school—so it was embarrassing that it took THAT long to get a freakin' box for us on a stupid test. Of course, we all knew it was monumental that this had happened at all. Until this happened, we had been checking whatever boxes we liked—White, Black, Hispanic, Pacific Islander, Native American, AND Other. I HATE that word—Other. I'm not an "Other"! I'm a mother, sister, aunt, daughter, sister-in-law, friend, Christian, educator, singer, and a darn good cook. I am NOT an "Other"!*

Stating she is not an *Other*, Selena describes herself, clearly stating what she is. Like Selena, I describe myself as a mother, sister, aunt, daughter, sister-in-law, friend, and educator. I'll pass on the singer and darn good cook.

What are some terms that describe you?

_____

_____

_____

_____

Unlike Selena, I've never had to look at the box that stated *Other* and wonder if I should check it. I always automatically checked *White* on any and all forms throughout my six decades of life.

As a middle-class, white female, and the mother of mixed-identity children, I have always experienced the privilege of knowing in what racial-identity group I *belonged*. My identity development consisted of figuring out who I was as a white girl growing up in the 1950s and 1960s. Both my parents were white and Catholic, so there was no tension surrounding race and religion. However, my dad was a Republican, and my mother was a Democrat, but we didn't discuss politics as a family. From my earliest memories, I was clear on my racial identity and don't recall experiencing a racial-identity development. I didn't have to since I was part of the dominant group in this country. My identity was mirrored back to me each day in every way, including all that comprised my educational context.

What does racial-identity development mean in today's educational context? Please share your thoughts below.

_____

_____

_____

_____

When I first thought about what racial identity means in today's educational context, I had no answer. I didn't know. As I read research and interviewed students and adults who shared their racial-identity stories, I learned more of *what I didn't know I didn't know.*

One thing I learned is that children whose parents identify differently, both racially and culturally, face challenges about which I knew little. How can I as an educator better support these students?

RACIAL-IDENTITY DEVELOPMENT MODELS

Think about how you constructed your identity. Does anything stand out? Did you try out different identities, particularly during adolescence?

_____

_____

_____

_____

Like all students, our multiracial students construct their own identities, but added to this construction of identity is the challenge that these students have parents who self-identify as different races. For example, one parent identifies as black, and the other identifies as white or whatever races with which they identify. Because one's parents identify as belonging to different races, some mixed-identity students feel they must choose one racial identity over the other. Pressure to choose one racial identity over the others is usually most intense during the adolescent years.

How do we develop a racial identity? Researchers have constructed models of identity development to better explain the process. Each model includes descriptive labels for the various identity choices and also includes the influences of the broader social context such as geography, generation, sexual orientation, gender, and class. In addition, the family, community, and physical appearance impact identity development (Root & Kelley, 2003, p. 39). However, Rockquemore and Laszloffy (2005) assert in *Raising Biracial Children,* "healthy racial identity for mixed-race people is less about which *racial label* a person chooses and more about *the pathway* individuals travel toward their identity" (pp. 18–19). The pathways vary from individual to individual as evidenced in the variety of pathways taken by the writers of the narratives in this book. As you read their stories, remember each person included is a unique individual who can't be generalized onto an entire group of mixed-identity people.

Mixed-students' identities may continue to be fluid throughout their lives, depending upon their individual experiences, and for us to assume they only identify as one race or a single identity does them a disservice. Observing, listening, and understanding, rather than classifying or stereotyping, allows us to better support our students. Nearly all of the persons interviewed stated they self-identified differently at different stages of their lives.

Read the following two narratives. Both are stories of teachers who describe their racial-identity process.

Alicia Cooper, pseudonym, White/Black, Born 1973
Teacher, Colorado
Written narrative

I was born February 23, 1973. My birth certificate does not state my race on it. I still have the forms my mom filled out when I was born. Under the area for race, my mother wrote White and Negro, the preferred terms at the time. My family in general did not talk about race. I had no idea that there was this perceived difference by society between Black, White, and Mexican.

I don't remember being aware of anyone's race or ethnicity or how they looked until I entered school. I remember my first day of kindergarten. There were a lot of tears, as there are with most kindergarteners. The only difference was that my tears were from fear and sadness from one particular blonde little girl in my class. I don't remember her saying very nice things to me. I don't remember the exact words, but I started to get a sense that I was some how different. I remember the shock that I felt when I found out that how I was different was a problem—a big problem for some.

I did not feel acceptable, but I was not sure why? When I found out that I was Black and the negative connotation that was associated with it, I became very upset. I came home and told my mother that God had made a mistake. I felt as if I had a disease. I think I may have asked my mother why she married a Black man.

I have always been a very driven person, even as a child, so I set out to make myself not Black for several years. Sadly, my efforts were reinforced by my White peers throughout my years in school.

Ideas that I had as a child included the following:

- *I thought that I was not smart enough in first grade (repeated first grade) because I was Black.*
- *I often did not believe what my mother said about race because she was White; she had the preferred skin color. I did not. My father never discussed race.*
- *My mother always told me that I was just Alicia nothing else. While she was correct the issue that I was dealing with in school never seemed to be addressed or settled.*
- *I thought if I married a White man, I would be accepted. I thought that our children might be so light that no one could tell that they had a Black background.*

Situations that I went through include the following:

- *I tried to scrape off my skin. (Around age seven)*
- *My Black cousin Nicole asked me if I chose to be Black or White. I told her that I was White. (Around age 10)*
- *I tried to bleach my skin with real bleach! (Around age eight)*
- *I wore very white make-up—I looked very silly.*

I got so tired of dealing with conflict that I would just pretend that it did not exist. I could only handle so much. Kids would say to me, "At least you're not as dark as those other Black people, gross." Kids would say, "You're pretty for a Black person."

[In college] when I took a sociology class, there was a class discussion about racism and inequality. The class was filled with around 50 students or more. I remember a young White man raising his hand and speaking out saying many things.

The main point that I got from his statements was that he was not racist; he had nothing to do with racism, and he basically had no reason to understand or care about racism. Well, this statement was it for me. For so many years, I had done whatever I could so White people (the preferred race) would accept me.

As he spoke, many situations ran through my head, including things that I knew about regarding my father. The fact was that he could barely read or write because no one in Mississippi cared if a black child did. In some situations, I heard about people saying, "They did not want the Nigger around," whenever my father entered the room.

The pain that I perceived my father as having and the pain that I felt throughout the years of my life came to the forefront of my mind. Tears began to fall. I was so upset that I went and talked to my teacher about the situation after class (she was Mexican); she just kind of looked at me like, "Duh! Don't you know that?" Or maybe she did not know what to say to me. Either way, she did not help me.

That was the moment I began hating White people. I had gone from one extreme to another. I changed my whole life based on this. I broke up with my White boyfriend. I moved to Denver. I stopped associating with my White friends on a regular basis. My focus was to be around just Black people. I found that not all Black people accepted me, but it did not matter. I could at least understand their dislike for me because I had felt the pain of ignorant White people inflicted upon me for most of my life. In their hatred, I felt their pain. I had gone through what they had. I went through hating White people for several years. I even hated my mom. It felt good for a while. As time went on and I was around more and more Black people, I started to calm down. I was not so angry anymore.

After several enlightening situations in my life, I decided that if and when I meet the man of my dreams, he may or may not be Black, which was my preference. I accepted that. As life worked out, I met Scott. He is Black, light-skinned Black like me. Most of our ideas about life as a people, as a Black people, as light-skinned Black people, complement each other quite well. Scott, however, thankfully does not have the type of experiences to draw up on that I do. He had a strong family unit.

When I came to the elementary school where I teach, I found a teacher that I loved to observe. She was White. She seemed to welcome me with open, loving arms. I knew that I wanted to learn from her. She kept her students engaged as well as physically and emotionally safe, which was all that I ever wanted growing up.

Next, I was so shocked and amazed when equity *started being discussed. After student teaching and experiencing equity training, I knew that this school was nothing like the schools I went to. Many of the teachers at this school care for and love all of the students. Being at this school has helped heal many pains that I felt as a child because I don't have to see another child go through it. I like the thought that they are in safe and nurturing environments.*

I am a work in progress. Through my life experiences so far with regard to race, I feel as if I have found my niche in life—who I want to be and how I want to conduct myself. I'm not constantly trying to change myself to fit what others would like for me to be. I feel that I am very good at respecting others' rights to have their feelings about themselves and me as they grow and transition at their own rate. The great part of it all is that we never stop growing and transitioning.

Alicia says she is a work in progress. I believe we all are. What do you think Alicia learned about herself as she sought her racial identity?

_____

_____

_____

_____

Currently, Alicia does equity work in her school district as a way to support other educators in their journey to understand the challenges that mixed students face. Her road to self-identity was long and difficult as she struggled to find her identity.

This broader social context is obvious in the narrative Selena shares below. At the beginning of this chapter, Selena shares she is not an *Other*, and in the remainder of her story below, she states in the first paragraph,

"I am multi-racial." Through her narrative, we learn what that means in her life. Note: Selena is a child of the 1980s, so keep in mind how the social context of her time shapes her story.

Selena Shade Jiménez, Multiracial: Black/White/Cherokee Indian, Born 1981
Teacher of Spanish, Chapel Hill, North Carolina
Written narrative

My legal name is Selena Shade Jiménez. My birth name is Selena Dare Shade. I was born in Hickory, North Carolina, on May 24, 1981. I am the fourth of five children. My father is Black, and my mother is White. My father's grandmother on his mother's side is full-blooded Cherokee Indian. In short, I am multiracial. I am the only child with red hair, a few freckles, and I have the fairest skin. Growing up in the Piedmont area of North Carolina was, to summarize, an experience. I don't remember growing up and being different *because we lived in the suburbs and were surrounded by a variety of people. I recall once that my father was building a new deck on our house, and he had a few of his friends over to help him over the month it took to finish the project. I remember his friends being all shades, no pun intended, and I now realized how well they all got along. I VIVIDLY remember times that we didn't "all just get along," such as the time my sister and I got barred from a community pool because she got into a fight with a* Redneck *boy who called her a* Nigger. *She beat his ass, and I STILL smile about that! I had no idea what was going on until it was all over. I also remember being called* Oreo, Mutt, *and even* Nigger.*

I went on to college at University of North Carolina-Chapel Hill. I was surrounded by diversity. I learned how to be myself, which was, at that point in my life, a 300-pound, redheaded, Black female. I had visited UNC many times before, but what made me attend was the last event they invited me to. It was called Project Uplift. As the name implies, the university invites rising high school seniors with a GPA of at least 3.5 who are minorities. We stayed at UNC for four days, and we engaged in life as a UNC freshman. We lived in the dorms, and we ate in the dining halls. We had sessions about what the university experience would be like no matter where we went; we had a going away event where a few of the Black fraternities and sororities performed for us, and we danced the rest of the night away. This single experience was the deciding factor in my decision to attend UNC. I remember entering UNC as a freshman in August of 1999 and seeing some of my Project Uplift session mates and being excited to start that chapter with them.

Every August, I begin the school year with an introduction of myself. In past years, I had a tri-fold presentation poster that I updated yearly as my nieces and nephews grew, and as I gained new ones. I recently made a PowerPoint presentation instead of updating the poster. I, being a very computer-literate person, chose to do it this way to save time and money. I give my presentation to the students the very first day of school, and I give it ENTIRELY in Spanish. I've found that the PowerPoint is helpful because I know everyone can see it. We go over the presentation the next day in English, but you'd be amazed at how many of my students go through the year without knowing my heritage or race. Of course I get asked, "What are you?" To which

I answer what I stated before . . . "I'm a mother, sister, aunt, daughter, sister-in-law, friend, Christian, educator, singer, and a darn good cook." I usually get to about the third or fourth thing, and they interrupt me by saying, "No, no, no! You know what I mean! What ARE you?!" I correct them and say, "You mean, what's my ethnicity?" And they say, "Yeah, your ethnithity [sic]" or they say, "Yeah, your eth—whatever!" (I intentionally spelled it incorrectly because most of the people who ask me this question can't pronounce it because they've not had to use it very often. I know this because I've later asked them why they didn't just ask me that in the first place.) I later explain to them how uneducated and rude they sound when they ask someone that question using those specific words and hope, as they go away with one bit of knowledge, that they use it the next time they find themselves in that situation.

When I started teaching at my current school in August 2003 after graduating from UNC in May, I had NO idea what lay before me. I distinctly remember a day during my first year teaching when I was showing a video in class. I had made it clear that the students should be paying attention to the video, and if they weren't, they were going to get another assignment, apart from the one they already had with the video. I saw a student writing and not paying attention, so I asked her to put away whatever she was doing. She didn't hear me because of the movie, so she proceeded to give me her notebook she was writing in. After school, I looked in her notebook and saw a letter she had written to her friend. She spoke about how my class was "so boring" and that it "sucked." She had also written a description of me. She said, "I . . . looked white, talked Black, had red hair, and spoke Spanish. How g**damn weird!" She later wrote me an apology letter explaining how insensitive it was for her to have written such a thing, but I can't help but think about all the students whose notebooks I didn't get to read. . . .

I identify myself as a multiracial female. I can pass *for White, Black, and even Hispanic if I need to. I sometimes feel guilty about* passing, *but it has always been what society has taught my siblings and me that we need to do in order to* make it. *I don't recall what I marked on the last census, but I will put Black if there isn't a biracial or multiracial box. I have come to this decision because I've always been told that, when in doubt, you are what your father is. I also feel guilty because I am, in my opinion, equal parts of my mother and my father. Many people think I am a Lumbee Indian—not White, Black, or anything else. I can pass for Latina if I speak Spanish, and it's even easier to pass for any of these on the phone.*

My husband and I had the discussion of "Do you want children when you're married?" when we were dating, so when we got married, it was a no-brainer. *We had our daughter, Ava Aleksandra Jiménez, on June 20, 2007. Now, you're probably wondering where Jiménez came from. Well, my husband is from Tabasco, Mexico, and it's one of his two last names. We decided I'd take Jiménez and move my maiden name, Shade, to my middle name. I didn't want my children to have a different last name than me, so my daughter only got Jiménez, and not Jiménez Shade, which is what it would have been if we followed the Latino culture's custom. My husband is Mexican but does not follow many Mexican customs or stereotypes, especially in terms of our daughter. We didn't have a baptism party; instead, we followed my family's customs and had a nice dinner with my family. Her first birthday is coming up, and we decided to go all out—carne asada, souvenirs, and even a piñata. She's having a party with my family, a.k.a. The Rainbow Coalition—my Black and White friends and colleagues, my husband's Mexican and Salvadorian friends, my White friends with Mexican husbands and biracial children, and my multiracial daughter.*

I recall one of my white friends with a Mexican husband and a biracial child asking me if her son was considered biracial or just Mexican. She asked because I made sure my daughter's birth certificate said multiracial. *I don't know what she put on her son's, but I let her know he is biracial, and if there wasn't a box for him that he'd have to decide what to put—just as I did and still do. When I asked the nurse, who went over the information on the birth certificate with me, if I could get multiracial, she said, "I guess so . . . I've never had anyone put that!" I explained my ethnicity to her and my husband's, and her birth certificate reflects all of that. I recall my husband saying quite a few times, "I hope she doesn't have your hair." I too hoped she got good hair so she wouldn't have to go through all the hassle that my sisters, I, and even my mom—she fixed our hair and put perms in it—had to endure.*

Salena Shade Jiménez elaborates,

I've never been told I have good hair . . . . I have red hair—it's really red, orange, yellow, and brown. I've NEVER dyed it and have been told it looks like a copper penny, a firecracker, and even Kool-Aid! My hair is REALLY thick, and I used to hate it when I was younger because I was different. My brother and my three sisters all have dark brown and black hair. My father's father had red hair and grey eyes, which is where I was always told I got mine from. I don't really like my hair when I desperately need a perm because I look like Simba from The Lion King. *When I'm introduced to someone Black who doesn't know I'm part Black, the person introducing me usually says, "You couldn't tell by her hair she was Black?!" I also have students that ask me, "When are you gonna get a perm?!" When I wash my hair and don't blow-dry it, it is wavy and some say I look white. It's never nappy, but when I was younger, I remember it being like that. MANY people ask me about my hair. The most interesting way someone asked me about my hair was, "Is that your real hair?" I knew they meant, "Is that your real hair COLOR?" and I answered, "Yes." Most people follow up with, "That's BEAUTIFUL!" or "Really?" It seriously happens on almost a daily basis—especially after I've gotten a perm. The most common way folks ask is, "Is that your natural color?" I've even had* professionals *not believe me until they look at my scalp, the hair on my arms, and my eyebrows. I vividly recall getting burned MANY times on the tops of my ears by the hot comb that my father put on the stove and then on my hair in order to straighten it so I wouldn't look like Simba.*

I am excited to make sure my daughter is comfortable with her multiracialism and to help her embrace ALL of it with pride, acceptance, and love.

Selena rejoices in her mixed identity. Share your thoughts about what you read.

_____

_____

_____

_____

WHAT I LEARNED?

- Multiracial students exist today at a transitional moment in history.
- I've learned that mixed-identity students go through a process of development that differs from monoracially white students.
- Racially mixed people call into question one-dimensional categories of race.
- This process differs because of the artificial racial categories used in our country.
- Since these mixed individuals do not neatly fit into any of the monoracial categories, they develop their identities in different ways than I, a monoracial individual, do.
- There are numerous models of identity development.
- Mixed-racial-identity development is a lifelong process, and mixed-identity individuals may identify differently at different times in their lives and even in different circumstances.
- I keep the same identity throughout my life.

What have you learned?

_____

_____

_____

_____

TAKING IT TO THE CLASSROOM— STRATEGIES TO BUILD COMMUNITY AND IMPROVE INSTRUCTION

- Consider having a _final five_ talk in your class. This means you hold a general discussion during the final five minutes of class at least once a week. This allows you to get to know your students better and see how they identify themselves.

- Use interactive journals in your subject matter. When students write their thoughts in journals, they tend to share more of themselves. This is another method to learn how your students identify themselves.
- Use goal setting. Have students set academic goals and personal goals at the beginning of each grading period. Goal setting improves performance and gives you a window into the students' minds.
- Incorporate *coming of age* stories into your curriculum. These stories are about adolescents as they develop their identities. They give you an opportunity to discuss identity development with students.

What successful strategies do you know?

_____

_____

_____

_____

I now understand there is a racial development process. I want to learn more about how racial identity affects students' perceptions of themselves. I want to learn more about how they experience the identities they choose or feel are theirs.

In this chapter, we examined the racial-identity development of mixed-identity children. In Chapter 6, we journey outside the school walls and learn from a professional who specializes in working with students of mixed identity.

SUGGESTED RESOURCES

Rockquemore, K. A., & Laszloffy, T. (2005). *Raising biracial children*. Lanham, MD: AltaMira Press.

Root, M., & Kelley, M. (Eds.). (2003). *Multiracial child resource book: Living complex identities*. Seattle, WA: Mavin Foundation.

6

Reaching Out to Other Professionals to Learn What I Don't Know

In this chapter, our journey takes a detour and invites the words of a professional in a field outside my realm of experience. Kim Anderson is an expressive arts psychotherapist who specializes in cross-cultural practice. She describes below how we met. We have continued our relationship because of our shared interests of equity and writing (and also of good food). We've spent many a meal together discussing our beliefs, assumptions, and responses to life's challenges. We have collaborated on many projects, portions of which are the topography of this journey and future ones that illustrate the interplay between individual professional development, classroom instruction, and effecting change in communities and beyond.

The reason I asked Kim to share her experiences of working with mixed-identity children is because she knows things *I don't know I don't know.* I understand the mixed-identity experience is not better or worse than other identity experiences (Spencer, 2006), but it *is* different. Kim shares valuable information on how children—who *have* been referred to a therapist—experience their identity. These children are experiencing issues larger than the usual *growing-up* issues. Because these children are in our classrooms, I need to learn about their experiences, too. But I also realize that I cannot generalize the information found in this chapter to all mixed-identity students; instead, I will use this information to build my background knowledge. In addition, Kim shares her personal story of categorization and how that affects her practice as a therapist. In doing that, she models the disclosure we find throughout the book that continues to guide our journey.

Kim Anderson, MSW, LCSW, ATR-BC
White woman, half-century in age
Expressive Arts Psychotherapist, Clinical Supervisor, Consultant, and Educator

The Universe has propelled me along Life's journey without much of an external guidance system. Often, destiny and detour have converged. Meeting Bonnie Davis was no doubt one of those combined crossroads.

I have never been sure what possessed either of us to take a mystery writing class, but that is where we met. We discovered how many other things we had in common: small-town Missouri roots, big-time dreams, conservative families, liberal attitudes, prison volunteerism, multicultural consciousness, love of good music, in love with good musicians, disappointment in bad food service, passion for good food, distaste for whiners, delight in good wine. We were leaving our primary livelihoods at about the same time. Bonnie was retiring from teaching; I was closing a twenty-year psychotherapy practice. We were both arriving at intersections of change and had no idea what was around the bend.

Bonnie's first book, How to Teach African American Students: Building a Classroom of Excellence *(2001) was a self-published labor of love of which I was pleased to be a part. She was clear in her vision of what was lacking in the literature for educators, and I was clear that my child clients could benefit greatly from teachers who were informed and culturally competent.*

Bonnie and I had many a conversation about her first book, and we continue to have courageous conversations *about the issues of race, the shifting cultural composition of the country, and the importance of helpers and educators keeping current with trends and being self-reflective in their practices. She asked that I, too, contribute my own personal and professional point of view to this journey toward how to teach biracial and multicultural students.*

As a licensed clinical social worker and board certified art therapist, I have expertise in multiculturalism and particular experience and enjoyment in treating very young children. I relish the purity, join with the fluidity, and encourage the divergence of young hearts and open minds. The mind and emotions of a child are boundless. The younger the child, the fewer limits imposed upon imagination, creativity, and acceptance (Craig, 1983; Gardner, 1995). Children ask questions to illicit that which is possible—not to confirm what is amiss. This, I think, is how the world should be: rich in honesty but open to fantasy.

I am a very white woman with very noticeable facial scars. It is not uncommon for my child clients to accept me as part of their culture, whatever that may be. If pressed for a definition, they will often decide that I am biracial. I am not, but I am honored by this adoption into their extended, blended families; it is testament to their unobstructed vision and an instinctive recognition of the color wheel within our internal and external therapeutic work.

What physical features do your students notice about you? What are their comments or questions?

_____

_____

_____

_____

How do you respond to their comments or questions?

_____

_____

_____

_____

When Bonnie asked me to share my own story and insights into the inner lives of multicultural and mixed-race children, I was excited to do so. This leg of the journey requires a balanced and steady step. As Bonnie discusses in Chapter 4, biracial and multiracial children have often been pathologized by clinical professionals who did not choose to admit what they didn't know they didn't know. _Although the expertise I share comes primarily from my caseload as an expressive arts psychotherapist, my practice has always been predicated on a strong belief that most all emotional and behavioral issues are rooted in psychosocial problems—social difficulties affecting psychological wellbeing. I look for external solutions rather than internal character flaws._

Many of the children I see come into therapy after their parents have been urged by teachers, school counselors, or even administrators to seek professional help for their child. Attention, behavior, and "attitude" problems are often the stated reasons. Demographically, my caseload is culturally varied. In my clinical work with these children and their families, themes reveal themselves: confusion, longing, familial dissonance, intolerance, aesthetic prejudice, and self-defeating patterns. These issues are not unique in therapy, but in many specific cases considered for this chapter, race, ethnicity, culturally blended families, and culturally based aesthetics contribute greatly to each client's reason for seeking treatment (Sue & Sue, 2003). As someone who specializes in multicultural issues, I receive these referrals.

Consider the terms "behavior disorder", "bad attitude", and "uppity". Which students come to mind when you think of these terms? What are the cultural and racial backgrounds of these students?

_____

_____

_____

_____

Each individual child or family arrives in my office with an agenda of correcting behavior or adjusting "attitude." These terms have become code words for me. Behavior problems *often arise when a child feels he or she has no other recourse. Frustration, anger, and fear often culminate in destructive actions toward persons or property, sometimes toward oneself.* Bad attitudes *tend to be a child's way of achieving passive resistance and escaping overt punishment. The emotional consequences may be just as damaging and self-destructive as bad behavior. "Uppity" is a word reclaimed by Maya Angelou (1978, 1983) but still used to shame girls and young women of color for not conforming to a self-defeating cultural* norm.

Do you see gender differences in how multiracial students are treated by their peers? What do you observe about the girls? How about the boys in your class?

_____

_____

_____

_____

Confusion may be stated in Why? *or* Why not? *questions. The children grapple with perceived day-to-day injustice and are bewildered by the unfairness. They may have attempted to verbalize their feelings to no avail. They resort to negative behavior to show discontentment.*

Each child indicates and manifests a deep longing to be understood and accepted for who he or she is in the here and now. For the children, the push for achievement is ever present, whether academic, behavioral, or attitudinal. Some level of grief is present for each.

While culturally blended families are created out of appreciation for differences and common bonding, difference frequently gives way to dissonance and dysfunction. In-fighting and rejection, especially when overtly based in racial assumptions, is as distressing and detrimental as peer or societal bigotry (Neace Page, 2002).

Intolerance mirrors intolerance. As it becomes clear to children that they are not tolerated, they in turn reject those who are intolerant. They also begin to internalize intolerance and become impatient with and rejecting of themselves.

I ask my clinical supervisees to consider this: Think about the child who is least like you. In what ways do you differ?

_____

_____

_____

_____

What are some things you don't know about this student? How could you learn?

_____

_____

_____

_____

Having once worked primarily with women and young girls, issues such as body image and aesthetic challenges were regularly discussed within the context of therapy. As my work shifted to children and multicultural families, I began to witness the effects of a different kind of body dysmorphia—an inability to accurately assess one's own physical presence. Size, weight, and perceptions of beauty are still represented, yet in multicultural contexts, these are accompanied by racial and ethnically defined dissatisfaction with appearance and presentation. Skin color, hair, facial features, carriage, and speech are also criticized and the rejection of them is internalized. This aesthetic prejudice reaches beyond the client and includes his or her choice of peer group, friends, and dating partners.

These themes culminate in a powerful clinical quandary and present a potent reality for which there is neither diagnosis nor prescribed treatment. Internalized racism is not an illness to be medicated but an often unavoidable societal condition.

What do you think about the term internalized racism? If you are an educator of color, have you ever experienced this? If you are a white educator, have you ever experienced white guilt?

_____

_____

_____

_____

While recognizing that race has become a very controversial term (Smedley, A., & Smedley, B. D., 2005), the word still exists in the tenets and codes of all major clinical professions (American Psychiatric Association, 1998; National Association of Social Workers, 1999; U.S. Department of Health and Human Services, 2001; American Psychological Association, 2002; American Art Therapy Association, 2003; American Medical Association, 2006; National Alliance of Mental Illness, 2007; National Association of Social Workers, 2007; Transcultural Nursing, 1997–2008). In addition, many of these sources define the term internalized racism.

My first professional organization, National Association of Social Workers (NASW), defines internalized racism as "the development of ideas, beliefs, actions, and behaviors that support or collude with racism against oneself" (National Association of Social Workers, 2007).

Bivens (1995) expands on this definition by stating that internalized racism involves at least four essential and interconnected elements: (1) decision making, (2) resources, (3) norms and standards, and (4) naming the problem.

Other outcomes of internalized racism may be seen in individual relationships, parenting, group efforts, leadership, isolation from like others, internalized stereotypes, narrowing of ones own culture, self-mistrust, immediate gratification, learning and long-range goals, survival, vulnerability to other oppressions and divisiveness (Lipsky, 2007).

Bivens (1995) also discusses cross-racial hostility. "Hostility is created in a racist system when one oppressed racial group supports the oppression of another oppressed racial group by supporting, benefiting from, maintaining, or participating in the set of attitudes, behaviors, social structures, and ideologies that undergrid the dominating race's supremacy" (p. 2). Bivens (1995) asserts that "racism is white people's problem, cross-racial hostility is the problem of people of color" (p. 2).

How do you feel about Bivens' assertion that "racism is white people's problem; cross racial hostility is the problem of people of color"? Give examples of each if you can.

Cultural Competence

Cultural competence *has become the standard for all health and mental health professions. Cultural competence is essential to proficient clinical work with individuals whose heritage, culture, ethnicity, environmental, and socioeconomic status are dissimilar to our own. M. Elizabeth Vonk (2001) cites McPhatter (1997) in conceptualizing cultural competency as the following: (1) enlightened consciousness, (2) grounded knowledge base, and (3) cumulative skill proficiency.*

NASW standards for cultural competency in social work state that cultural competence "refers to the process by which individuals and systems respond respectfully and effectively to (all) people . . . and protects and preserves the dignity of each." Five essential elements contribute to the ability to become more culturally competent: (1) valuing diversity, (2) capacity for cultural self-assessment, (3) be conscious of the dynamics inherent when cultures interact, (4) institutionalize cultural knowledge, and (5) program development that reflect an understanding of diversity between and within cultures (National Association of Social Workers, 2002).

My other primary professional organization, the American Art Therapy Association, includes "multicultural awareness" in the ethics document, "Ethical Principles for Art Therapists" (American Art Therapy Association, 2003). Similarly, the American Medical Association, the American Psychological Association, American Psychiatric Association, and the U.S. Department of Health and Human Services have statements of standards regarding proper treatment of diverse populations.

Do your professional organizations require training in multicultural awareness or cultural competence? What do you gain from participation in these trainings?

_____

_____

_____

_____

How Does This Help the Children?

When sitting with any of my clients, I experience the work we do on three distinct planes. I teach my clinical students and supervisees about these therapeutic planes: the Here and Now, the Real World, the Re-Created Life. I believe this model may be translated to work in the classroom.

The Here and Now is about what happens during each session. In educational terms, it might be called a teachable moment. *Where do we start? What do we learn about one another? What does that teach us about how to be more comfortable in the world? and How can we put what we learn to use in the Real World?*

Describe a culturally based teachable moment that occurred in your classroom.

_____

_____

_____

_____

The Real World is the world outside of therapy or teachable moments. It is in the home and in the classroom, in the lunchroom and at baseball practice. How does therapy (or a positive classroom experience) influence our behaviors and attitudes in the rest of our lives? How can we change negative patterns into positive practice? How can we stop ourselves from regressing?

How have you been influenced by your experiences with multiracial students? How does this show up in your life outside of school?

_____

_____

_____

_____

The Re-Created Life encompasses all that we become during our therapeutic or educational time together. If we change/learn, who will we be next? Will we be accepted by our friends, our families, and society? Fundamentally, will we be happier, healthier? Will we continue to grow after we leave the office for the last time or graduate from school?

Imagine your own Re-Created Life. Describe what that would look like a year from now. Five years. Ten.

_____

_____

_____

_____

What Does This Mean for Us As Helpers/Educators?

In prefacing these examples, I write as we. My personal/professional experience grows and changes along with my clients. In clinical terms, this is positive parallel process. In the Real World, this is self-awareness. In all helping professions, self-awareness is the foundation for multicultural awareness and cultural competency (Saleebey, 1994).

A developmental model of cultural competence is made clear by Bennett (1993) via six stages moving from ethnocentric stages of denial, defense, *and* minimization *to ethno-relative stages of* acceptance, adaptation, *and* integration.

Consider Bennett's six stages of cultural competence. Where do you place yourself along this continuum? What keeps you from moving through the other stages?

_____

_____

_____

_____

I think about my own journey of self-discovery and awareness. I began, rather ignorantly, as a white woman whose only claim to diversity was that of gender bias. Joining clients in their travels during the years, I have come to realize that my aesthetic challenges—my obvious facial scars—give me early entre to cultural acceptance. I, too, am seen as different—sometimes as less than, sometimes as more than I should be, sometimes as "uppity" for daring to be in the Real World, Re-Creating my life day by day.

As I walk with Bonnie along this journey, I am once again pleased to stroll in step with her as she clears a path of debris and clutter of the cultural biases in our society's history. This is a difficult but essential road. Because of the generosity of those who share their stories, all who follow can travel with a little less baggage, more awareness, and the courage to walk the talk.

WHAT BONNIE LEARNED

- *Bad attitudes* tend to be a child's way of achieving passive resistance and escaping overt punishment. The emotional consequences may be just as damaging and self-destructive as bad behavior.
- Each child indicates and manifests a deep longing to be understood and accepted for who she or he is in the here and now.
- Intolerance mirrors intolerance. As it becomes clear to children that they are not tolerated, they in turn reject those who are intolerant. They also begin to internalize intolerance and become impatient with and rejecting of themselves.
- *Internalized racism* is not an illness to be medicated but an unavoidable societal condition.
- Internalized racism is "the development of ideas, beliefs, actions, and behaviors that support or collude with racism against oneself" (National Association of Social Workers, 2007).
- Internalized racism involves at least four essential and interconnected elements: (1) decision making, (2) resources, (3) norms and standards, (4) naming the problem.
- Hostility is created in a racist system when one oppressed racial group supports the oppression of another oppressed racial group.

What have you learned?

_____

_____

_____

_____

In this chapter, we sought knowledge from Kim, who resides outside the school walls. On our journey to equity, racial literacy, and cultural proficiency, we listen to the voices of other professionals; and in this case, we listened to Kim. In Chapter 7, we learn how skin color categorization has been a part of our national landscape for many years and what effects it can have in your classroom today.

REFERENCES AND SUGGESTED RESOURCES

American Art Therapy Association. (2003). *American Art Therapy Association ethical principles for art therapists.* American Art Therapy Association, AATA Board of Directors. Reston, VA: American Art Therapy Association.

American Medical Association. (2006). *Code of medical ethics of the American Medical Association.* Chicago, IL: Southern Illinois University Schools of Medicine and Law.

American Psychiatric Association. (1998, December). Diversity. *Position statement.* Washington, DC: American Psychiatric Association.

American Psychological Association. (2002). *Guidelines on multicultural education, training, practice, and organizational change for psychologists.* Washington, DC: American Psychological Association.

Angelou, M. (1978). *And still I rise.* NY: Bantam Books.

Angelou, M. (1983). *I know why the caged bird sings.* NY: Bantam Books.

Bennett, M. J. (1993). Towards ethnorelativism: A developmental model of intercultural sensitivity. In R. M. Paige (Ed.), *Education for the Intercultural Experience* (pp. 21–71). Yarmouth, ME: Intercultural Press.

Bivens, D. (1995). *Internalized racism: A definition.* Boston, MA: Women's Theological Center.

Craig, G. J. (1983). *Human development.* Englewood Cliffs, NJ: Prentice-Hall.

Gardner, H. (1995). *Developmental psychology.* Boston, MA: Little, Brown, and Company.

Lipsky, S. (2007). *Internalized racism.* Retrieved June 18, 2008, from The International Re-evaluation Counseling Communities: http://www.rc.org/.

National Committee on Racial and Ethnic Diversity. (2001). *NASW standards for cultural competence in social work practice.* National Association of Social Workers. Washington, DC: NASW Press.

National Alliance of Mental Illness. (2007). *Cultural competence in mental health care.* Washington, DC: NAMI.

National Association of Social Workers. (1999). *Code of ethics.* Washington, DC: NASW.

National Association of Social Workers. (2002). *Equity: Practice update on cultural competence.* Washington, DC: NASW.

National Association of Social Workers. (2007). *Institutional racism and the social work profession: A call to action.* Washington, DC: NASW.

Neace Page, M. (2002, August 8). *Reactions in the field: Interviews with helping professionals who work with biracial children and adolescents.* Cincinnati, OH: University of Cincinnati.

Saleebey, D. (1994). Culture, theory, and narrative: The intersection of meanings in practice. *Social Work: Journal of the National Association of Social Workers, 30*(4), 351–359.

Smedley, A., & Smedley, B. D. (2005). Race as biology is fiction, racism as a social problem is real: Anthropological and historical perspectives on the social construct of race. *American Psychologist, 60*(1), 16–26.

Sue, D., & Sue, D. W. (2003). *Counseling the culturally diverse: Theory and practice* (4th ed.). NY: John Wiley & Sons.

Transcultural Nursing. (1997–2008). *Cultural competency.* Retrieved June 18, 2008, from Cultural Diversity in Nursing: http://www.cuturediversity.org/cultcomp.htm

U.S. Department of Health and Human Services. (2001). *Mental health: culture, race, and ethnicity—A supplement to mental health: A report of the Surgeon General.* U.S. Department of Human Services, Substance Abuse and Mental Health Services Administration, Center for Mental Health Services. Rockville, MD: Substance Abuse and Mental Health Services Administration, Center for Mental Health Services.

Vonk, M. E. (2001). Cultural competence for transracial adoptive parents. *Social Work: Journal of the National Association of Social Workers, 46*(3), 246–255.

Wadeson, H. (2000). *Art therapy practice: Innovative approaches with diverse populations.* NY: John Wiley & Sons.

7

The Impact of Skin Color

Few would deny that skin color is important in this country. Why is skin color so important? It is important because it has assigned value and affords privilege to those with white skin. When my son was growing up, I used to try to figure out just what it was that made others see him as black. Was it the shape of his nose, his hair, or his skin color? I'm not sure of the answer in his case, but the fact his skin color is darker than what most define as *white* makes a difference in the way others categorize him. And since skin color is an external, physical attribute, we can use it to classify others into groups of the powerful and the not so powerful.

What color is your skin? Does it give you power?

_____

_____

_____

_____

Has your skin color robbed you of power? Have you been stopped by the police because of your skin color? Refused service in a restaurant? Passed over for a position? I know none of these things has happened to me. Others have stories that differ.

Our journey brings us to the issue of skin color and an attempt to learn more about how skin color impacts our classrooms. For example, what decisions, knowingly or unknowingly, are made based on skin color? Are positions in our schools ever based on skin color? Is tracking based partly on skin color? Educators may deny it, but it is worth examining. Using skin color as a basis for categorization is not new; it has been occurring for a long time in this country.

THE LEGACY OF SKIN-COLOR CATEGORIZATION

Categorization based on skin color has a long history in this country supported by forefathers such as Thomas Jefferson. Thomas Jefferson supported the emerging Black and White racial caste system by advocating the development of a U.S. Census (Singleton & Linton, 2006, p. 160). He wrote about white superiority and black inferiority in *Notes on the State of Virginia* (1781) and called groups existing between the two *mulattos*. He suggested that *mulattos* could eventually become White, but Blacks lacked the intelligence and genetic properties to ever become White (quoted in Singleton & Linton, 2006, p. 160). Other categories were created and implemented at various times throughout our history.

Even though Americans now have the option not to identify solely as White, Black, American Indian, Asian, or Pacific Islander, this is not a new phenomenon, as stated above. In the past, the categories of *mulatto, quadroon,* and *octoroon* existed to relegate people to positions of lesser power and privilege. In addition, people who wrote *biracial* or *multiracial* onto their census forms were lumped into the *other* categories until 2000. The 2000 Census was the "first decennial census to allow respondents to self-report their multiple racial identities by selecting one or more races, and as such, marked a significant milestone for multiracial people" (Jones & Smith, 2001, p. 4).

What did you mark on the 2000 Census? Did you know the 2000 Census was the first time respondents could self-report their multiple racial identities?

_____

_____

_____

_____

In the 2000 Census, 6.8 million people, 2.4% of the U.S. population reported more than one race (Jones & Smith, 2001, p. 4). The self-designated multiracial population is diverse and young. About 42%, or 2.9 million were under 18 years of age with nearly 70% of all multiracial people being younger than 35 years of age and only 5% of the multiracial population reported being 65 years or older. About 25% of the population who reported one race was under 18, and 12% of the population reporting one race was over age 65 (p. 5). Clearly, more younger people than older people are self-designating multiracial identities. The 2000 Census was a historical census in self-reporting, and it was followed by a historical election in which a man with a mixed-race heritage was elected President of the United States.

Do you think the 2000 U.S. Census breaks down racial barriers or further entrenches the concept of race? How and why? Share your thoughts below.

_____

_____

_____

_____

Skin color categorization continues to change. This was a surprise to me, but it's true. Gunnar Myrdal (1996), in his book, *An American Dilemma*, pointed out more than 50 years ago the browning of black people. A person the census taker in 1850 might have judged as a *mulatto* would have been judged as black in 1920. In brief, as the entire *Negro* population became lighter, people who were thought to be black and those who were thought to be *mulatto* became lighter; therefore, *mulattoes* were counted as blacks in increasing numbers. "Black Americans cover the phenotypic gamut, and affirming a multiethnic ancestry and being *Black* are not mutually exclusive. Claiming Blacks to be monoracial in this country is historically false, and the 30 million African Americans are already mixed" (Spencer, 2006, p. 101).

Teachers may be unaware skin color can cause tension between students in the classroom. What implications does this information have for your classroom?

_____

_____

_____

_____

SKIN-COLOR TENSION BETWEEN MIXED STUDENTS AND MONORACIALLY IDENTIFIED STUDENTS

Is there ever skin-color tension between students? Unfortunately, the answer is yes, and it tends to be more prevalent among females. Skin color prejudice is more prevalent in females because the worth of a female is tied to her physical appearance (Rockquemore & Laszloffy, 2005, p. 146). You only have to look at the magazine covers at the nearest store to see that light skin is valued over dark skin in our society as evidenced by the sheer quantity of covers featuring light-skinned women. Hopefully, this will change as First Lady Michelle Obama and other women of color grace the covers of leading publications. Yet presently, it is no surprise that we may have internalized the racist message that white skin is superior to dark skin, and the ideal beauty is one who possesses white skin, blonde hair, and blue eyes. As a result, if we possess white skin and/or blonde hair and blue eyes, we may feel a false sense of superiority to those with darker skin, and this false sense of superiority may translate into our body language and cause hostility from those with darker skin with whom we interact.

How does this affect mixed-identity students? Since mixed-identity students have been acculturated in a dominant culture, which in this country is white culture, they may find themselves more closely identifying with white people and internalizing this false sense of superiority. Rockquemore and Laszloffy (2005) find "when light-skinned girls internalize the white supremacist valuation of light skin, it can be devastating to their relationships with dark-skinned girls" (p. 146). So much so that they suggest that biracial women be aware of their own gestures that may be viewed as hostile by darker skinned girls. For example, a flicking of the hair can provoke hostility. The flicking of the hair is a gesture that seems to "personify the historically rooted sense of superiority of those who approximate a white beauty standard" (p. 147). Yet when I do workshops on race, I seldom find a white woman who is aware of the implications of this gesture. To learn more about this gesture and its impact, consider reading the chapter on hair in *It's the Little Things: Everyday Interactions That Anger, Annoy, and Divide the Races* by Lena Williams (2002). As I continue my journey to racial literacy, I find that reading books such as this one inform me about *what I don't know I don't know.*

Skin-color tension sometimes arises between mixed-identity females—not defined as black by others—and females defined as black. Several of the females interviewed share incidences when they were ridiculed or shunned by students of color who had darker skin than they. Diana Breckenridge shares the skin-color tension she has experienced.

I threaten Black women. I will become the center of attention in an intimidating way, and if there are men around, the women become more aggressive. They see me as threatening, more so than a White woman. It's blacks and people who are different from Caucasians. White people are comfortable in their own skins. It's time that all people feel comfortable in their own skin, but it's still very installed in black people that they are second-class. So when there is someone who is black and mixed with white, that can be very intimidating.

Even though Diana shares that she believes she threatens black women and they sometimes become aggressive towards her, she confides that she is still more comfortable socializing with people of color than with whites.

The issue of skin color is complicated, and this chapter just touches on the issue. The examples in this chapter center around mixed-identity female children with one white parent and one black parent and the tension arising from their relationships with black women. There are additional issues surrounding skin color, including the denial of its value. However, skin color preference exists throughout the world. Lighter skin usually receives privilege and power over darker skin.

How will you use the information on skin color to inform your classroom practice?

_____

_____

_____

_____

Alicia describes her skin color as "golden," and this chapter ends with her narrative. Alicia Edison's academic work centers on race. She wrote her masters thesis on biracial children, and she is currently a doctoral student writing about race. Alicia believes that "race is an artificial concept (i.e., social construct), but again, its effects are real." She adds, "Until race has no political or emotional power, we should still discuss it. This is not and will not be a colorblind society for a very long time."

Alicia Edison, Biracial: White/Black/Blackfoot Indian, Born 1982
Doctoral Student, Manhattan, Kansas
Written narrative

I am a-third-cup French, one pound German, one-fourth-teaspoon English, a pinch of Blackfoot Native American, two cups Irish, and three tablespoons African American. Cook at 350 degrees for one hour and get ME! This process of finding the me has been a long and trying process. I wasn't always this confident in who I am. Now, I get a clear sense of who I am and where I am going. I am a biracial woman who is a multiracial activist. I am a lifelong student and a future teacher.

My story begins in Germany. My father was in the Army, and my mother was in the Air Force, and we were stationed in Augsburg. Those stationed on the Army base came from everywhere—Puerto Rice, Guam, and all over the United States. Color and race meant nothing; we were all Americans stationed in a foreign land serving one country.

[We moved to Wisconsin, and] my mom enrolled my sister and me in a small rural school. As the new kid, I already felt different. I tried my best to fit in, and at first, I did. The kids in my class initially wanted to play with me, and I was everybody's new best friend. I was invited to ice skating shows and sleepovers. This soon changed when their parents found out that I was Black. I no longer was invited to anything. I was not played with during recess, and I became the object of ridicule during lunch. My teacher and the other staff did not help me. They told me not to play with them and not to talk to them. That wasn't the problem. They were already doing that to me. I was heartbroken and alone.

Luckily, I had three friends who looked like me. They were others like me. They were Native American and had brown skin like me. Unfortunately, my teacher separated me even from them when we had to take the annual standardized test at the end of the year. We were filling out the demographic information section. She told us to raise our hands when our races were called. She started off by asking if there were any Native Americans in the class. Three kids raised their hands. She asked if there were any Blacks in the class. I didn't raise my hand because I was looking for the golden box. My mom always called me golden so that is what I was. I didn't find my box, and my teacher pointed me out and said, "Alicia, you are Black. Check the Black box." I didn't know what that was. In Germany, color and race meant nothing. My parents never told me what that word meant. My teacher then asked the White students to raise their hands when White was called. Their hands flew in the air, and my heart sunk. My experiences at that school taught me Black was bad, and since I was Black, I must have been bad.

I was upset. I was angry and hurt. I didn't understand why my mother didn't teach me how to protect myself from people who were so mean and close-minded. I understand now that she didn't know better. She is a White woman from a small farming community with no diversity. At home, race does not matter. I am golden, and my parents love me no matter what. But sometimes, love doesn't solve everything. Love can't protect me from the world and how some people see me. At home, I am just Alicia. Once I walk outside the door, that all changes. Society tries to force me into a box, a box that labels me as Black. With that comes all the consequences of not being White in a society that considers White the ideal type and something to strive towards.

I should be bitter and hate White people, but how could I hate my mother? She is not like them, so I had hope in my heart that not everyone was like them. With the grace of God, my father survived Desert Storm, and we were relocated to Fort Riley, Kansas. In this town, I finally discovered my mixdar. This is a tool that I use to recognize other mixed people. I don't know what it is, but we mixies can recognize each other with just a glance. I finally felt as if I wasn't alone.

After high school, I went to a university on the opposite side of the Army base. Strangely, it lacked the diversity that my hometown had. It was predominantly White. I wasn't afraid that I would have similar experiences that I had in Wisconsin. After all, college educated people are supposed to be liberal and open minded, right? Well, that wasn't always the case. I bonded with other minority students, usually Black students, because finding other biracial or multiracial people was difficult. I didn't want to feel as if I were alone. However, I did get the question, "What are you?" occasionally from Blacks and often from Whites. I think because of what I look like, people initially have questions along with the need to categorize me. I happen to like the way I look. I am unique. I used to try to conform to Eurocentric standards of beauty by straightening my hair and style of clothing. These are the same standards held in the African American community. I don't think that I conform to those standards consciously anymore. I have cut my hair and grown it out naturally. I wear what is comfortable. If people don't like me for reasons based on my appearance, then it doesn't matter. They didn't know me to begin with.

Alicia writes about her racial-identity development and the impact of skin color and other phenotypes on her identity. Please write your thoughts about her narrative below.

_____

_____

_____

_____

Alicia shares her beliefs about race below. As you read them, consider your own beliefs.

When I am asked the question, "What are you?" I often tell the person asking the question that I am biracial. If they ask me what my mix is, I will tell them if their question is from a place of pure curiosity and nothing else. When I am asked this question, I think that it is another teachable moment. Most likely, that person is ignorant and has no idea that they are also constrained by society's labels of who they can and cannot be. I would like monoracial people to ask questions from a place of curiosity and not from a place that either confirms or disconfirms their preconceived notions about mixed people. Maybe they should try to get to know me on a more personal level outside of race, which takes time, instead of jumping into the very personal realm of racial identity. Because of my experience of trying to discover myself and why people in society perceived me the way that they did, I decided to write my senior thesis on biracial identity. I have been studying that ever since.

From my research and personal experiences, I have learned that biracial people do have more choices today than they did in the past. Biracial people can choose the identity society gives them as the race of the minority parent. A biracial person can choose a biracial identity, which incorporates both parents' racial identity. He or she can choose when to identify with either race with a protean identity, one that changes. A biracial person can opt out of the racial categorization game altogether and choose none. Whether the biracial person feels guilty depends on how educated he or she is about his or her own identity. As I learn more about this topic, the less confined I feel, the less I feel the need to make people feel okay with who I am, the less I feel as if I am the problem and need to change. Society needs to change, and slowly, it has. The language used to refer to biracial people has changed over time. For example, mulatto was used to describe a person who is mixed, usually with a Black and White background. This term is derived from the term mule because it was once thought that mulatto people could not produce offspring. When I was called a mulatto or heard the word around me, it used to upset me, but as I learned the history of the word, it made sense for that time period. Would I like to be called that word today? No, I would not. Does it have a huge negative impact on me? No, people and society just really know this term in reference to biracial people, if they know anything about biracial people at all. In my research, I have found that names for multiracial and biracial people have changed throughout history from mulatto, quadroon, and octoroon to Black. The one-drop rule has changed the way American society sees biracial people. They are not seen at all.

I want to be seen. I want others like me to be seen. Because of this, I am a multiracial activist. I am working towards a category for us—validation for us. I am often miscategorized. When this happens, I correct people and tell them what I am if they come from a place of pure curiosity and not a place of hate and judgment. I tell them, "Yes, I am Black, but I am also French, English, Irish, German, and Blackfoot Native American." Then I ask them what they are and usually they only can tell me that they are White or Black—nothing more. I find it funny when they are asking me what I am, and they don't know what or where they came from.

There are those who choose to not use racial terms altogether and profess that race is just a social construct. That is true. Race as a biological construct does not exist, but the consequences of it being a political tool does. Race isn't real, but racism is. Until racism is rectified, I believe we should acknowledge people the way they perceive themselves to be. Some argue that there have never been pure races and that all people are mixed. That is true. However, those who have parents of two different races experience the world differently than those who are monoracial. I believe my biraciality questions society's ideas of race.

I believe that before we can choose to be 100% of ourselves and validated for that, things like government forms and the U.S. Census need to change. When it comes to the U.S. Census, I choose Other. *I am not just one of the boxes that those in power have listed. On other forms, I either mark* all that apply *and* other *then write in what I define myself as, or refuse to answer at all. I guess it depends on how I feel that day. I define myself as* Golden. *This is what my mom calls me, and this is what I am. I am not just* Black. *I am not even considered to be* White. *Why can't I just check the box that says* Me? *I don't know when biracial and multiracial as categories will be validated. I do know that reality and this concept question society's ideas of race.*

The personal narratives offer a window into how race is embedded in our personal lives. Catherine Squires (2007) in *Dispatches From the Color Line: The Press and Multiracial America* suggests we take a "hard but nuanced look at how race is embedded in each person's life and what it means in the broader context" (p. 207). Reading the narratives and taking a hard but nuanced look at how race is embedded in each of the narratives can create a place for courageous conversations. These courageous conversations can be internal through our reflections or external with our colleagues. Please consider sharing your thoughts with others as we continue our journey together.

This chapter looked at skin color as one of the issues that challenge our mixed-identity students. Being aware of these issues better equips us to face situations that may arise and supports our understanding of the journeys our mixed students take as they navigate their way to identifying themselves.

WHAT I LEARNED

- In the 2000 Census, 2.4% of the U.S. population reported more than one race.
- The self-designated multiracial population is diverse and young.
- Black Americans cover the phenotypic gamut.
- Affirming a multiethnic ancestry and being *Black* are not mutually exclusive.
- Claiming Blacks to be monoracial in this country is historically false.
- Students usually want to see themselves reflected in their peers and desire diversity in classrooms.
- Skin color has power. I must continue to examine if I give more value to white skin than to dark skin.
- Skin-color tension can exist between mixed students and monoracially identified students due to issues of internalized racism.
- Skin-color prejudice may be more prevalent among females because of the emphasis on physical appearance.
- Skin color has power.
- Learning about issues about which *I didn't know I didn't know* broadens my capacity for understanding all the students in my school.
- Attaining cultural proficiency helps me recognize racism in its externalized and internalized forms.

What have you learned?

_____

_____

_____

_____

TAKING IT TO THE CLASSROOM: BUILDING COMMUNITY AND IMPROVING ACHIEVEMENT

- Post pictures of people of all different skin shades in your classroom.
- If teaching middle or high school students, build a classroom library of adolescent novels that deal with issues of skin color.
- If teaching elementary school students, fill your classroom with books that show children of all hues and colors.
- Have students do self-portraits and display them in your hallways.

- With older students, consider discussing racism in its externalized and internalized forms as it centers on the issue of skin color.
- Continue to reflect upon your own perceptions of skin color.

In Chapter 8, we listen to the voices of parents. These parents have children of mixed heritage. They share their personal stories with us in order that we may understand better how to educate their children.

RESOURCES FOR CONTINUING TO READ ABOUT SKIN COLOR

Gaskins, P. (1999). *What are you? Voices of mixed-race young people.* NY: Henry Holt and Company.

O'Hearn, C. (1998). *Half and half: Writers on growing up biracial and bicultural.* NY: Pantheon Books.

Rockquemore, K. A., & Laszloffy, T. (2005). *Raising biracial children.* Lanham, MD: Rowman & Littlefield.

Spickard, P. (1989). *Mixed blood: Intermarriage and ethnic identity in twentieth-century America.* Madison, WI: The University of Wisconsin Press.

Williams, L. (2002). *It's the little things: The everyday interactions that anger, annoy, and divide the races.* NY: Harcourt.

8

Parent Voices

Our journey brings us to the narratives of parents of mixed-identity children. I value their stories. As a parent of mixed-identity children, I seek out the stories of others who may share similar experiences. This chapter taps into the personal knowledge that parents gain as they nurture children of mixed identity.

BUILDING RELATIONSHIPS WITH PARENTS AND CAREGIVERS

We must find ways to build relationships with parents and caregivers. How do we do this? First and foremost, we build relationships with parents and caregivers by caring about their children.

I'm convinced parents want to know we care about their children. If parents don't think we first care about their children, they often choose not to engage in meaningful communication with us. I recall an incident that clearly illustrated this. I accompanied a parent to Open House one year at a neighboring high school. At the time, I was mentoring a freshman girl who was not doing well in most of her classes. Her mother was not happy with the performance of her daughter or with the teachers who taught her. We visited three teachers who met the icy stare of the mother with politeness then gave their dire reports on the daughter's academic progress. In contrast, the fourth teacher, the math teacher, welcomed the parent with this opening sentence: "I love your daughter!" The mother changed into a different person, relaxed her folded arms, and was ready to listen to what the teacher had to say. The teacher then went on to tell how he incorporated the daughter's strengths into his instruction. By the end of the conference, the teacher and the mother had devised a plan to support the academic achievement of the girl. Knowing that this teacher cared about her daughter caused the mother to care about the teacher and listen to what he had to say. The parents in this chapter care about you enough to share their personal stories of their children in order that you may learn about the challenges mixed identity brings to their lives. We educators profess we want parents' input; well, here it is. Read their narratives and enjoy.

I met Karen at a Newcomers club when I moved to California in 2005. I was immediately impressed with her intelligence and honesty. She wanted to share her story with us because she says she seldom has the opportunity to discuss the issue of race.

Karen Notarainni, White, Born 1959
Mother of Alicia, Adopted Brazilian Child, Houston, Texas
Written narrative

There is something bittersweet at finally assembling this collection of memories, anecdotes, and quotes that make up my current-day understanding of what it means to be a multi-ethnic family. Our uniqueness in this regard deserves the telling of the story. That being a multi-ethnic family is a story is somewhat sad to me, but that we are one is the basis for my husband's and my greatest joy. We adopted our daughter, Alicia, while we were living in Sao Paulo, Brazil, where my husband worked for the Disney Company. She was two days old the day she was placed in my arms. And so began our education into what it means to be a multi-ethnic family.

As we embarked into new situations, this provided new opportunities to grow in our understanding of diversity. When my daughter was three years old, she started preschool. One day she commented that she couldn't wait to be older, when her skin would get lighter. I asked her why she wanted her skin to be lighter. She told me that her preschool friend, Annalyssa, said, "lighter skin is better." As my heart sunk, I asked her, "Who is always complimented on the color of her skin—you or me?" "Me," she would answer correctly. I pointed out that if everyone had the same color skin, it would be like a rainbow in all one shade. I reminded her that rainbows are only beautiful because of the all the different colors. People are the same way. Happy with my inspirational analogy, we continued our walk.

It was about this time that I realized that I wasn't helping Alicia enough in matters of ethnicity. She knew she was Brazilian, that she was adopted, and that this made her and our family very special. I believed at the time that being open, honest, and accepting of all types of people spoke for itself. It doesn't. I realized that the picture books Alicia had in our home contained pictures mostly of blonde, blue-eyed children. Look again, for the first time, at the newspaper comics as though you had a child of color or ethnicity. Maybe you'll see what I suddenly saw. I couldn't get to the library fast enough. Bill Cosby's Little Bill *series of books is exceptional for children. We borrowed every single one over time and then borrowed our favorites of them again. These stories include challenges that children learn to overcome, lessons of kindness and sharing, and humor galore. I knew I was on the right track. At that young age, Alicia was permitted to watch only* Sesame Street *and* Arthur *on TV. Both programs contain the gamut of creatures in every shade. This was a pivotal moment for me in my own understanding of what I faced as the parent of this child.*

This worked handily until Alicia's first-grade year when she announced to me over dinner at Sweet Tomatoes that she considered herself black. She was studying Martin Luther King, Jr. in class. Her fabulous teacher, of East Indian origin, told the students that in Canada where she grew up, she was called "puddin' face" because of her dark complexion. This was the first time that Alicia expressed to me her struggle with understanding her own color in terms of those around her. She explained that she knew she wasn't white, so she must be black. This was where I shared with her the fact that the Portuguese language has many names for skin color, whereas the United States does not. I explained that skin color is treated differently in different cultures. It may happen some day that she may come across certain individuals who will say negative things about darker skin. I have reminded her many times that this says far more about the ugliness of that individual than it says about her.

I believe that it is germane to our Sweet Tomatoes discussion (and her declaration that she is black) that we lived in Phoenix, Arizona, where Alicia attended a school that was 79% white. As a parent, I heard longings from my daughter at this period how she felt different than others and that she felt that she stood out. She attributed this to the color of her skin, although it may have been exacerbated by her now recognized intelligence. This was the school that classified Alicia as gifted and talented and placed her in accelerated language and spatial relations classes. More important, Alicia identified her feelings of difference as skin-color related.

Her concerns about her skin color disappeared when we moved to Irvine, California, where she attended a school 42% White, 35% Asian, and 12% Hispanic/ Latino. Her first friends were Argentine and Pakistani. This was another pivotal moment in my understanding of diversity. My daughter feels more comfortable in the presence of greater diversity. Alicia would describe her friends to me in a variety of ways, straight-haired, eye color, and whether they were darker or lighter than she was, placing herself in the center of the color scale. There was no inflection or suggestion that any skin color was preferred. Being a multi-ethnic family among great diversity is very definitely less complicated than being among a more homogenous population. I believe that the children in this environment were more tolerant of cultures, races, and ethnicities also. Irvine, California, was a rarity where diversity and high scholastic achievement existed together. Usually, I am forced to choose diversity at the sacrifice of scholastic excellence or vice versa.

In 2008, my family and I moved to The Woodlands, Texas, a suburb of Houston, known for their very good schools. At the end of Alicia's first day of school in our new city, she told me that her school has a lot of straight, long-haired students. Within a week, her curly hair was referred to as an "afro," and she told me that people looked at her as if they were judging her by her skin color. My daughter's new school, made up of only fifth and sixth graders is 85% white. While I'm relieved that my daughter has fallen into a very diverse group of friends, Alicia told me of an incident that happened recently on school grounds. The girls were all trying to do splits. From a side group of girls, someone commented that she "didn't know fat, black girls could do splits." This black girl, who was the brunt of such unkindness, is also the one who has encouraged Alicia to respond with anger and loud words to similar girls who mock her curly, sometimes unruly hair. Alicia is unconcerned with what others say about her hair and said so to her friend. I think her black friend heard racial undertones in the hair remarks, whereas Alicia only heard unkind hair remarks. When you've been the brunt of racial put-downs, I think a person is quicker to hear racial connotations in nonracial remarks. Or I am naïve about the fact that the hair comments weren't racially linked? Whose reality is real?

Karen asks, "Whose reality is real?" How would you respond to her question?

_____

_____

_____

_____

You can read her daugher Alicia's narrative in Chapter 10.

Rufina Hernández works with Brenda, my grandbaby's mother. Rufina wanted to share her story and was anxious to share the importance of culture in her life and in the lives of her daughter and grandchildren.

Rufina Hernández, Chicana
Associate Director of the External Partnerships and Advocacy
**   Department of the National Education Association,**
**   Washington, DC**
Telephone interview

I am Latina, a Chicana, from New Mexico, and grew up in the southern part of the state, in Carlsbad. This part of New Mexico is "Little Texas" because it has a lot of attitudes similar to that of the Midland and Lubbock, Texas, areas, so it's sort of a derogatory term for that part of New Mexico. Most New Mexicans don't like Texans, so to call it "Little Texas" is meant as a dig to that part of New Mexico because some of the population act as if they are a part of Texas. Those attitudes are racist and sexist—racist towards Hispanics even though they're not a minority—even though whites are in the minority, the power was all held by whites. It's sexist because many still hold the belief that women are there for populating.

As a result, when I was growing up in the '60s and '70s (I graduated from high school in 1973), the Chicano movement was very strong in various parts of the country, but the southern part of New Mexico was very resistant to it. As a result, I am very assertive about being Chicana because I was resisting that pressure to conform, to assimilate, and not show any difference.

We were punished for speaking Spanish; we were segregated and not integrated until sixth grade. I grew up learning I was different, and it (speaking Spanish) was inferior. As an adult, I'm very proud of that difference, and I am not letting anyone intimate that I am inferior.

When my daughter, Francesca, was born, I hyphenated her name—Hernández-Lewis—because I never wanted her to pass as white. Because she is half white, she could pass if she chose. I made it a point that she would have to be identified by the virtue of her last name. I worked very hard on her to have her learn the customs and culture of the Hispanic community, teaching her Spanish, making sure she knew the different rituals and traditions and customs, the Mexican folk dances, many of the traditions we do during the year—the cultural value of family. I think that all came through ultimately. My first husband and I divorced, but the reason I was so aggressive about the Hispanic culture was because I thought she would just get the Anglo culture by default. She grew up in Denver and went to a Catholic school that was predominantly Anglo. I didn't think I had to work as hard to engender that cultural tradition. Then I remarried when she was three, and she now has a Black stepfather.

Rufina is concerned about her daughter learning about her culture. How does this differ from learning about one's racial category?

_____

_____

_____

_____

Curtis Linton is a working colleague of mine. Together we wrote, *No Excuses! How to Increase Minority Achievement* (in press). We do presentations and trainings together, and we share the experience of having children of mixed heritages.

Curtis Linton, White, Born 1974
Vice President, School Improvement Network, Salt Lake City, Utah
Written narrative

Transracial Adoption: Is Love Enough?

My wife and I are the proud and joyous parents of a remarkably buoyant three-year-old boy. We are White; he is multiracial: one half Black, one fourth Filipino, and one fourth White. This is known as a transracial adoption, where the child is of a different race than the parents. We adopted him at birth and cannot believe how much richness he has added to our lives. We know we love him dearly, and he knows this as well. But is love enough?

When our son is in our house, we can control how his world treats him. He is expected to be well behaved, achieve highly, be inquisitive, and learn all he possibly can. When he falls in our yard, we are there to comfort him. We can remove the thorns and rusty nails that might be found within our vicinity. He will learn about the heritage we come from and that he shares with his grandparents and cousins, and we will share about the incredible gift his Black birthmother granted when she decided to place him within our White arms. All of these things we can control. Under our guidance and care, he will be safe.

But what about when he leaves our home? What then? Will he walk out of our loving home into a school that only sees him as a Black boy? Will he be subject to racial prejudices that I have never experienced and only understand in the abstract?

One question we often ponder is where to send him to school in two years when he becomes five. One choice is to send him to a more diverse school outside of our immediate neighborhood where there are more than 50%

students of color. But that school is not as academically proficient as the school closer to our home. But at the closer school, he will be only one of a handful of kids of color. Interestingly, there will be other Black kids at the elementary school near us, but almost all of them are adopted by White families as he is. Then again, how well will Black kids accept him within their circles with his fairer skin, curly hair, and other less-Black features?

What is better? Racial similarity or academic achievement? How can I possibly understand the third culture he will experience? He isn't White but sure understands it. He isn't Black but sure looks it. These are the questions of a White parent of a transracially adopted child. We love our boy so very, very much. But what else do we need to know to provide him with everything, yes, everything, he needs?

What concerns does Curtis share? In what ways does his narrative enlighten you about parents' concerns about their mixed-identity children?

_____

_____

_____

_____

As you reflect upon your own work with parents and caregivers, what insights do the narratives offer you?

_____

_____

_____

_____

I met Kim Kouri in a workshop I did in Omaha, Nebraska. She wanted to share her struggles and triumphs of mothering children of color.

Kim Kouri, Lebanese/Italian, Born 1966
Teacher, Omaha, Nebraska
Mother to Children of Color
Written narrative

I grew up in a small, rural, highly conservative, Republican, Catholic community in northwest Iowa. The town had approximately six thousand God-fearing, hard-working people. My dad was a former high school chemistry and advanced math teacher who changed careers and decided to sell insurance. My mom was a former elementary teacher who could afford to stay at home and raise my younger brother and myself. We lived an upper-middle class lifestyle. We were blessed. I must add . . . my dad was full Lebanese with parents who were proud of their culture; my mom was mostly Italian. So . . . I'm biracial although I look white. I like being me . . . and checking the other box when asked about my ethnicity. I never understood why it is so important to document. Hmmm.

Anyway . . . back to the town I lived in . . . LeMars, Iowa. It really was a great place to grow up . . . it just wasn't too multicultural. Actually, I think our family was probably the most multicultural thing there. One year, we actually had an African American kid enroll in our school for a quarter. That was way cool! Unfortunately, he left. I never really knew anything about his family, why they moved to LeMars, why they left . . . anything. I just knew he was really awesome, and I liked having him in school. We did have a college, too. Westmar College, which eventually changed to Takio-Westmar. That really did not go over well in our culture-challenged community. Westmar did have black students. Once again . . . cool! I always felt as if our world was bigger than LeMars, and welcomed people of different ethnicities, backgrounds, and color. Don't misunderstand . . . people in LeMars were wonderful to our family . . . but every now and then someone would make a racist comment or joke (not directed at me—but black people), which was always so offensive to me. Plus . . . it made me wonder what people said behind my back . . . or especially my dad's . . . since he looks very Middle Eastern.

Creighton University. 1985. Wow! Talk about a culture shock . . . but I loved it! There were people from all over the United States and world, for that matter. This was really different from the little town I grew up in. I met, dated, and lived with a Hispanic man for almost three years. After a year of being single, I met Stacy. In August, I will have been with Stacy for 18 years. We have an unconventional relationship (technically, we are not legally married), not to mention a 16-year-old son, and a 12-year-old nephew (Stacy's sister's son), who we are raising. Stacy is biracial. He is black and white, and our son is BEAUTIFUL.

I enjoy having a culturally blended family. Granted, it hasn't come without trials and tribulations because it is ethnically blended, but we were able to deal with it. One incident happened when we were first dating. We were walking into a movie theater when a group of African American ladies shouted to Stacy, "Traitor!" That really bothered me. He said it didn't matter to him. He could date anyone he wanted, but it bothered me. Why would people say that?

Another incident took place in California with my son and his first-grade teacher. She was Mexican American but apparently did not like black people . . . or my son. She would make certain comments to my son about his dad and myself, and when we'd see her in public, she'd visibly frown as her eyes, darting them from the three of us and back and forth. It was one thing to treat me disrespectfully, but it was an entirely different ballgame when she started acting that way to my son. Again . . . what confused me was that she was a minority (by classification) too. Racism crosses boundaries and knows no limits to its evil.

Kim writes how racism crosses boundaries and knows no limits to its evil. Comment on her observation.

_____

_____

_____

_____

I met Glynnis in her store where she sells her art. She and I bonded easily as we shared stories of our families. Fortunately for me, she and her husband, Stan, a professor of musicology and African American studies, were kind enough to be interviewed and share with us.

Glynnis Breckenridge, White, Former Elementary School Teacher
Artist, Laguna Beach, California
Mother of Children of Color: Hispanic/White; Black/White
Transcribed face-to-face interview

When Stan and I were dating, 18 years ago, there was an incident in San Clemente, California. My child was heavily involved in a sport, and the parents of the other kids had known me for years. Once after a game, Stan and I were in the middle school parking lot, and he said goodbye and gave me a peck on the cheek. One of the mothers with whom I had socialized, yelled, "Goddamn nigger bait!" across the parking lot. I was so shocked. Her daughter, who was sitting in the back seat, had her mouth open with a look of amazement on her face. I'll never know whether that look of amazement was because I was with the n-word man or because her mother screamed out the window. At that time, this incident caused me to evaluate whether I was going to be strong enough to end up married to this person. It gave me a definite forewarning. I guess I decided yes. I still remember what I was wearing because it was such a shocking experience.

When I married my first husband, who was Hispanic, we had custody of his two children, five and eight years old. I realized right away that when I went shopping by myself, it would be a normal experience; but when I went to a mall with these children, there would be floorwalkers every time it seemed who would follow us. They were so obvious that we would often actually leave the store. I would go back in a week by myself, and there would be none of that. I took Chelsea, my daughter with Stan, to the mall when she was five. And she has about the same skin tone as the two children of my first husband's. It was in a Macy's, and I went up to a counter to purchase something, and an older lady (in her seventies) at the counter looked at me and smiled, then she looked down at my five year old and gave such a dirty look; her lip actually curled up, and she looked away from both of us. And I felt torn between my respect for older people and my urge to slap her. A cute little five-year-old girl. I decided to not say a word because then I would just bring it to my little girl's attention, and I thought she didn't notice it. A few hours later, we got into the car to leave the mall, and my little girl asked me, "Mom, why did that lady give me a dirty look?" Diana was a very friendly child, and she would be in a public place and say hi to someone or just walking and look up to her parent and say, "They did not say 'hi' to me. Why did they not say 'hi' to me?" And I realized by that point in time, a darker-skinned child is very tuned in to nonverbal cues.

I have blonde-haired, blue-eyed grandchildren. When I go places with them, they always receive smiles from strangers. When I've gone places with my dark-skinned children, rarely has there been a smile. And that smile usually comes from another darker-skinned adult. It is obvious to me as a parent and grandparent how much this affects a child's self-esteem even before he or she starts kindergarten. I also noticed this with my Hispanic children. When I was with my dark-skinned children, all I got were stares and a lot of dirty looks, and this started to wear me down.

In 2007, Diana and I were at a pet shop in Laguna Beach, California. We were adopting a little black dog. Diana is an obviously mixed-race girl. The owner of the pet shop referred to the dog we asked to see as her "little nigger." I looked at Diana; usually, she would blow her top. The dog's trainer looked at us in shock, but no one said anything. We were just out to rescue a dog.

In my daughter's middle school last year, the girls were giving themselves nicknames, and this girl asked my eighth-grade daughter, "Can I call you nigger?" Chelsea looked at her and said, "No." Hearing that was very upsetting to me. You don't escape those things even in the upscale area of Laguna Beach. I eventually told the principal, but Chelsea did not want to point the girl out.

Stan L. Breckenridge, PhD, African American, Born 1952
Lecturer, California State University/Fullerton, Laguna Beach,
   California
Father of Multiracial Children
Transcribed face-to-face interview

As a parent who happens to be a father, I think about the advantage that a biracial boy has over a biracial girl. Our society is not nearly equal where it should be regarding gender preferences. I tend to feel that for my son—he is accepted as a person, whereas for my daughter, she was accepted with the condition that she is part Black or part White. Sterling had the advantage of his name, his height, his personality. Sterling's name played an important part in how he was perceived by other people. Race didn't seem to really matter. Both of my children are very attractive. It's also interesting that my children tend to associate with different groups. Sterling tends to associate with White people and White women; Diana tends to associate with Black people and Black men. That could be because of what I said earlier; Black culture tends to accept a person in a more respectful way especially those we've been around, not to say everyone.

Diana, knowing the biracial heritage she has and aware that White teens tended to treat her in a more degrading manner, felt more comfortable associating with Black people. There is a double standard there because Black women tend to not like fair-skinned Black women—a separate issue there. Sterling associating with White people and White girls could also have to do with his or with a young man's association with his mother. A daughter associates with her father, and I tend to see that a lot in families in general, be they biracial or not. Sterling tended to associate with his mother; Diana tended to take on some of my traits. For example, Sterling was very good in art; his mother was very good in art also. He played saxophone; he was interested in what I did but seemingly excelled in what his mother did. Diana excelled in music; she also did art, but she gravitated towards music. I wonder if it was because of her association with her father.

I don't think racial attitudes have changed as much as the fact that the change is more in me. Because racial discrimination is not new to me, I have changed, which makes racial offenses less poignant than when I was with

Sterling and Diana when they were young. I was impatient with other people's impatience. When I would get a look from someone, black or white, mainly white, I may have taken offense in my 20s and 30s—lack of ignorance on both parts. My opinion is just as valuable as theirs—what really does it matter?—these things I had to acquire. As I think about (my daughter) Chelsea and what happens today, in one sense, it has seemed to have gotten better because of how I think; on the other hand, I have become more educated and wiser in knowing how to combat some kinds of negative attitudes that someone is giving her and/or me, and I tend to have the ability to discern much more easily and quickly. Therefore, because I can see it more quickly, I don't internalize it; I just say yes or no, and no longer wonder if this is how they really feel. It doesn't affect me for a long period of time. In my 20s or 30s, what seemed to be a negative look could affect my entire day. Which is so foolish—now, I realize certainly that is not important.

As you reflect on the parents' and caregivers' narratives, what insights do you have regarding working with the parents of your mixed-identity students?

_____

_____

_____

_____

You can read their daughter Chelsea's narrative in Chapter 10.

I met Graig Meyer at a National Staff Development Conference in New Orleans where we participated in Glenn Singleton's Beyond Diversity training. Graig's courageous conversation continues to educate those with whom he works; he shares his experiences as the father of a teenager of mixed identity.

Graig Meyer, White, Born 1974
Educator, Chapel Hill, North Carolina
White Father of Adopted Biracial child
Written narrative

During her third-grade year, I accompanied my daughter Ashley's class to a play. Before the performance, I was sitting between my Ashley and a classmate named Ashlee. The other girl was the class outcast. Poor, unkempt, and socially awkward, she was the kid that no one else wanted to sit next to. I'm drawn to those kids, so I was happy to sit with her and be her conversation partner.

As I talked with Ashlee about whatever nine year olds like to talk about, I could tell that my Ashley was growing impatient. Not only was her dad talking with someone else, he was talking with the one person that no one was supposed to talk with. Ashlee soon made an abrupt transition. "You know what's funny," she started. "Her name is Ashley, and my name is Ashlee. She's black, and I'm white." "I'm biracial," was the immediate response from my right. Ashley had whipped her head around me, her neck stretched to its limit, and her eyes glaring. I knew it was time to refocus my attention. And it was time for some discussion about identity.

Yes, Ashley is biracial. I'm white. So is my wife. Ashley is adopted. When she joined her family at age six, we had a lot to learn about race. She had lived with her white biological mother but had never known her black biological father.

When you adopt a child, one of the things that you're taught is how to help the child tell their own adoption story. Indeed, almost right away Ashley needed to be able to explain that she was adopted. In first and second grade, her classmates would regularly look at me, turn their puzzled looks to her, and then spit out some form of, "Is that your dad?" that always made it clear something didn't fit.

Of course, it was race that tipped them off, but at that age, the conversation didn't readily go there. Ashley's practiced adoption story at that point was pretty simple. "Yeah, I'm adopted." When pressed, she could add, "My biological mother couldn't take care of me so I came to live with my new parents." On the day of that third-grade field trip, it became clear that the issue in question was not adoption. It was time to help Ashley convert her adoption story into a story about race.

"I'm not black. I'm BIRACIAL." That statement is loaded with so much baggage. How do you help a nine year old pick it apart? To start with the first half of the statement, we had to examine why it was so important to Ashley that she make it clear that she wasn't black. Initially, her response was that a third Ashley in their class was the black one. She wanted to distinguish herself from both of her like-named peers. But of course, children that young can learn the power of race and internalized racism along with it. With white parents, it's saddening but not surprising that our young daughter would exhibit signs of such.

It would be naïve to see the vehemence behind Ashley's statement as based in pride. It was clear upon utterance that she was rejecting her blackness. Remember that it had been prompted by her white classmate's racial comparison—"I'm white; she's black."

Ashley's response stung me when I heard it. Even as a white parent, I was keenly aware of the internalized racism inherent in the statement. Flooded with complex feelings, my thoughts flew. We hadn't done enough to make her comfortable being black. She didn't know how to talk about her race. My own racism even played out in briefly blaming Ashley for dropping a racial dialogue bomb, when clearly her white peer was equally involved. What a mess. It's been a struggle since her adoption to help Ashley find strength and pride in her blackness. In fourth grade, we had advocated for her to be in a program for academically gifted students, and once she got in it, she wanted out because there were no other kids who looked like her. In sixth grade, she told us with confidence that white kids are smarter than black kids.

It has been difficult to ensure that Ashley gets identity affirmation in school. Now in high school, there is still a shortage of high achieving black kids in her school. When she is in advanced classes, she's often one of three or fewer kids of color. In school-related settings where there are more black kids (such as the track team), academic success is often de-emphasized.

To counter this pressure, we've tried to make sure Ashley is enrolled in some of the many special programs designed to support achievement among African American students. Like any youth organization, some have been better than others. The best are ones that provide a space where students like Ashley can work together to build positive identities, spaces that support the image of blackness that Ashley's godparents emphasize: strong, intelligent, and independent.

Let's go back to the second half of that statement. "I'm BIRACIAL!" Just as Ashley had developed an adoption *story earlier, she needed a* biracial *story. I hated adding to her burden of always having to explain herself, but her life's path had been cast. We needed to help her deal with it. "Ashley," I began later that evening, "I don't think that Ashlee had any idea what you're talking about. Do you remember when we taught you how to tell your adoption story? It's just like that. People don't understand just by looking at you and me. They need us to give them more information."*

There was a point when she was about seven that she got a huge identity affirmation while at the beach. Looking at lots of tanning white women, she said to her mother, "Look, they all want to have the same color as me." It's always been easy to emphasize the beauty of her skin color because people tell her how beautiful she is all the time. But biraciality is about culture as much as color. Her color cues people to ask questions or make assumptions. But what's always harder for her to explain (and maybe to understand) is her relationship to black culture as a kid growing up in a white family. To help her develop her biracial story, we had to dive deep into this story. We had to figure out how to help a nine year old understand why white kids wouldn't identify with her because of her skin color, but black kids wouldn't identify with her because of how she speaks and acts as well as who her parents are. Really, it was a conversation about her whiteness.

The specifics of that day's conversation elude me after seven years, but in truth, it's a conversation that has never ended. There have been so many examples of times that we've rehearsed her responses to peers who push her on identity issues.

There have been times in sports, such as when two black girls in her gym class told her that they were sitting out the tennis lessons because tennis was for white girls. Perplexed, Ashley brought that one home for discussion. She easily pointed out the success of Venus and Serena Williams. But the deeper struggle was about why the girls would sit out and risk failing to make a stand about racial identity. This struggle can't be pulled apart from the idea that white kids care more about school success.

As the parent of any biracial kid knows, identity issues come up all the time in issues of dating. My favorite example came in eighth grade when Ashley started breaking down the complex rules of who gets to date whom in her class. Her description was entirely about white and black kids. I asked her, "Who do biracial kids get to date?" She replied, "There's a Brazilian boy I think is cute." A creative but ultimately unfulfilling answer, she knew she wasn't going to get white racial privilege or black cultural currency in the dating game.

For most of those tough middle school years, her biracial story went something like this: "I'm biracial, but I'm also adopted, and my parents are white." The most common reply from her peers was, "So are you black or white?" Ashley would roll her eyes and say, "Both." Almost any other question, such as, "Why do you talk like a white person?" would be met with another eye roll and a typically preteen, "I don't know."

The world is confused by her. People know she's not white. They also know she's beautiful. What she never knows is what other assumptions they harbor based on her skin color. I'm sure her story will continue to evolve over time. I just hope that the world's view evolves with her.

Most adoptive parents know that some day their child is going to drive a very specific stake through their hearts: "You're not even my real parents." Intellectually, this is a preposterous statement to hear from a teenager, but both parties know that it carries huge emotional weight. Adopting Ashley transracially, we knew that she'd also have another zinger up her sleeve one day: "You don't understand because you're white." The two sledgehammers actually came within close proximity to one another. During a period of struggling with a daughter in her early teens (which is not uncommon for any parent-daughter relationship!), Ashley tried to use both of them within a week. The adoption line really hurt my wife. I played it off by telling Ashley it didn't hurt because we'd always known she would say it at some point. Still, internally, I was lamenting losing my secret dream that we would good enough parents that she would never say it!

But the "you're not black" line really was a laugh. At this point several years later, I can't remember the exact situation that precipitated it. But when it came up, I literally laughed in Ashley's face. That didn't help the situation given her percolating anger. But I quickly pointed out that my understanding of whatever she was complaining about was based on being her parent and not my (or her) race. It was true, and her argument was foiled. Still, I made sure to bring it up again. Later when heads had cooled, I made a point to tell Ashley that race was not something that should get in the way of us understanding one another.

Graig says the conversation never ends. In what ways does Graig's narrative illustrate courageous conversations about race?

_____

_____

_____

_____

You can read his daughter Ashley's story in Chapter 10, *Future Voices.*

The parents' voices in this chapter offer us much to think about as we continue our journey. Each parent has his or her own set of experiences; just as every parent of monoracial children has unique experiences.

What additional insights have you gained from reading the parents' narratives?

_____

_____

_____

_____

What are your thoughts after reading the parents' narratives?

_____

_____

_____

_____

When I think of my own experience as the mother of mixed-identity children, several things emerge. First, when my daughter Leah was growing up, I didn't confront the kinds of feelings I did when my son Reeve was a child. Leah looked white, and we lived in a white social world. With Reeve, however, I found I acted in ways I had not acted having a little _white_ girl in a mostly white setting. Since Reeve stood out as being different in my neighborhood, church, and social group, I found I tended to have the following characteristics:

- I was hypersensitive to any remarks about my son and second-guessed others' motives.
- I was overprotective and did not want my son going certain places and doing certain things because of his skin color.

I also found that I wanted the following:

- To learn more about other cultures
- To be included in and accepted by persons of other cultures

Some of these are positive, such as wanting to learn about other cultures, but others placed additional stress on my family as I attempted to navigate in territory where I did not have a map. Fortunately, my son's dad is an understanding man who is a stabilizing force when dealing with issues of race, and he often set me straight about what _I didn't know I didn't know._ I also benefited from my friendships with women of color, such as Dorothy Kelly who shared her racial history in my earlier book and continues to share personal experiences and cultural knowledge with me.

I share the above because I think it is important to recognize there was no _how-to manual_ (back in the 1980s) for the mother of a mixed-identity child in our society. As do most parents, I did the best I could, but I wish I had done many things differently.

What similarities do you find in the parents' narratives?

_____

_____

_____

_____

How do the parents' narratives differ?

_____

_____

_____

_____

WHAT I LEARNED

- Parents of mixed-identity children face different experiences from parents of monoracially identified children in addition to many that are the same.
- Parents of mixed-identity children want the same things parents of monoracially identified children want for their children.
- Parents of mixed-identity children must create spaces for courageous conversations about race.

What did you learn?

_____

_____

_____

_____

TAKING IT TO THE CLASSROOM

- Invite parents into your classroom. I found when I taught seventh grade, it helped immensely to have a parent in the classroom.
- Invite parents as guest speakers to share their stories.
- Find ways to expose the strengths of the students. Publicize, post, and publish the positive things the students do!
- Have students do oral histories of their parents and grandparents and caretakers.
- Hold a writers' showcase where students read their oral histories for their families. This can be done during the school day, perhaps in a library. See a detailed description of how to do this in my book, _How to Teach Students Who Don't Look Like You: Culturally Relevant Teaching Strategies_ (2006, pp. 129–130).
- Hold a potluck dinner one evening at the school and invite the families of your students.

SUGGESTIONS FOR WORKING WITH PARENTS AND CAREGIVERS

- Express to parents and caregivers your concern for their children. Show them you really care.
- Ask parents and caregivers to share any information about their children they think might benefit you as an educator.
- Ask parents and caregivers' *advice* on what they believe is best for their children.
- Suggest alternative meeting places and times for parent conferences to accommodate everyone's schedule.
- Ensure that your conversations with parents and caregivers are conducted with the utmost respect in regards to cultural mores. Learn about the cultures of the parents and caregivers and the students.
- Be warm and kind and smile.

As educators and parents, we try to do our best. Sometimes we don't succeed. But as parents when we feel our children's teachers really love our children and want the best for them, we are so much more ready to partner with them; and as educators, when we feel our parents really care about the work we do, we are so much more ready to work with them. This chapter gives us insight into the realities some parents face so that we may continue our work to be more empathetic towards all our students to understand the things we don't know we don't know about the lives of others.

In this chapter we heard from the parents. Now it's time to take this to the classroom. In Chapter 9, we learn classroom strategies suggested by the adults and students interviewed for this book as well as my own suggestions based on the research.

SUGGESTED RESOURCES

Root, M. (2001). *Love's revolution: Interracial marriage.* Philadelphia, PA: Temple University Press.

Spickard, P. (1989). *Mixed blood: Intermarriage and ethnic identity in twentieth-century America.* Madison, WI: The University of Wisconsin Press.

9

A Call to Action

Culturally Proficient Suggestions and Strategies

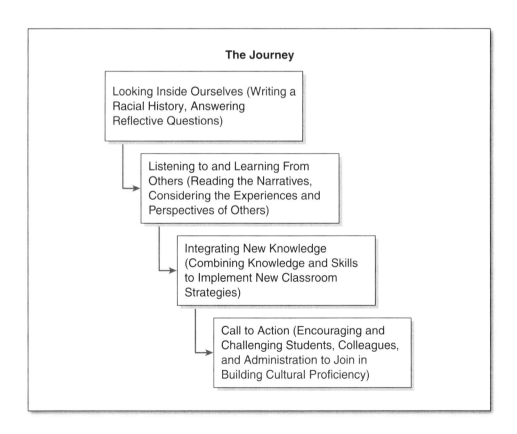

The Journey

Looking Inside Ourselves (Writing a Racial History, Answering Reflective Questions)

Listening to and Learning From Others (Reading the Narratives, Considering the Experiences and Perspectives of Others)

Integrating New Knowledge (Combining Knowledge and Skills to Implement New Classroom Strategies)

Call to Action (Encouraging and Challenging Students, Colleagues, and Administration to Join in Building Cultural Proficiency)

Our journey brings us to the classroom, and it's time to step inside and specifically address classroom instruction. We've read and reflected. Now we need action. What can we *do* that supports the achievement of our mixed-identity students? Answers are in this chapter. I am so excited to share suggestions with you that come straight from the educators, parents, and students interviewed for this book. These are suggestions shared in their own words and based on personal experience. In this chapter, we address Step 3 in the preceding flow chart. It's time to integrate new knowledge by combining knowledge and skills to implement their suggestions in our classrooms. As you read their suggestions, take small steps and focus on one to three suggestions you will commit to implement on your journey to cultural proficiency and racial literacy.

How do we discover the information we want to know? In workshops, when teachers ask me what to do in certain situations in their classrooms, I often reply, "Ask the kids." Sometimes the very information we crave is what the students are dying to tell us. After all, who knows more about how they feel than they do? In writing this chapter on what teachers and educators can do to improve educational experiences for mixed-identity students, it seemed only natural to ask the multiracial educators who contributed to this book to offer their suggestions. Drawing from their own educational experiences, they offer you a myriad of suggestions and strategies for consideration. In addition, there are additional suggestions from professionals who work in varying capacities with mixed students and from the students themselves.

As you read these suggestions and strategies, consider which will work for you. It is up to us to reflect upon new information and make the final decisions concerning how we might implement what we learn to meet the needs of the students in our classrooms.

First, think about the strategies that already work for you. What strategies do you use?

_____

_____

_____

_____

You already use the strategies listed above. Now you can add to your repertoire. Below are the suggestions individuals shared.

Note: The responses that follow range from stories to lists. We each have a preferred style in which we want new information delivered. Some like lists; other prefer anecdotes. I practice cultural proficiency when I listen to individuals using the communication styles they choose rather than insisting they share in my preferred style.

I asked the following question:

What suggestions and strategies do you have for educators who want to meet the needs of mixed-identity students?

Karen Hayes, African American/White/Blackfoot Native American
Associate Professor, Department of Educational Administration and
**   Supervision, University of Nebraska**
Omaha, Nebraska

I loved my little country school where all the children looked like me and where the teachers who looked like me told me I could grow up and also become a teacher or anything else I set my mind to becoming. I knew way back then that I wanted to be a teacher so that I could be just like the teachers that I had. My teachers were warm, friendly, cared about me, maintained high expectations, and knew me well. They knew what I enjoyed, and they knew how I enjoyed learning. They took the time to help me feel important and special. I yearned to attend my neighborhood school because I was being educated in an environment that loved me. I believe my teachers perceived themselves as being a part of my extended family. They made learning fun, and connected our learning to our prior knowledge. We had opportunities to shine in class, and we were in an environment where we felt safe to fly!

I believe teachers today need to become more culturally responsive to their students. They need to build relationships with their students and maintain high expectations with continuous support to be successful. They need to provide safe environments where students know that they are able to be successful and that it's good to be smart and capable, and if they don't know something, the teachers will provide the resources and support to gain the information needed for success. Teachers should know if their students have special interests and abilities such as music, art, drama, and so on. And if the children have not discovered their special gifts and talents, teachers need to provide opportunities to discover or rediscover the joys of their strengths, gifts, and talents.

Schools should seek to build on the knowledge that students bring; many children of color are extremely resilient and understand way more than they are given credit. To exist in a society that seldom recognizes the talent and beauty that a person of color holds means that the child has had to learn to survive very creatively against many difficulties that many white adults would struggle to understand.

Jacqui Felgate, White
Teacher, Rockwood School District
Rockwood, Missouri

In my professional life, as a teacher, each new school year brings a new bunch of students. I find myself in the same position; the students in my class need to know what I am, which always leads to "Are you Black, Hispanic, Indian—from India—or Middle Eastern?" I just smile and explain that I was born in the United States; I am German, Irish, and Italian. Some of the students have the "Oh" moment when they hear the Italian, some just wanted to know just to know. I do feel that it somewhat brings me closer to some of my students because I do look different than most of the teachers that they see throughout the day. I have grown to understand that not all people feel comfortable with people who look different, but if you feel comfortable with yourself that is the only thing that matters.

Joe Rousseau, Oo'henumpa Lakota/Cherokee/Irish/German
Teacher, Middle School Science
Lincoln, Nebraska

The path to becoming familiar with the dominant culture's subjective curricular facts is where I find a place to provide the students with the space to explore and create their own identity. Interacting with others within the classroom community of learners, listening to others' ideas, comparing them with our own perspectives, and growing through this shared experience, at our own pace, with our own methods, utilizing our individual strengths, creating a final product within which all have contributed to, is much more beautiful than we could have created on our own.

Alicia Edison, Biracial
Doctoral Student
Manhattan, Kansas

I am a teacher and one day will be one professionally. As a person of mixed race, I would like teachers to take into consideration that biracial students are like any other student in the class. To make the biracial student feel included and validated, the teacher could have multiracial and multicultural literature available. In this way, biracial students can see themselves and monoracial students can see students who look different from themselves. Another strategy that teachers can use is to celebrate differences through activities and cultural celebrations. This includes monoracial groups as well. Diversity and celebration of diversity is what is important. One thing teachers should avoid is to assume that any behavioral, academic, or emotional problem is due to the student's racial background. Teachers should also avoid assuming that the biracial student identifies with the minority parent or any racial identity at all. To help achieve the goal of cultural celebration, teachers can be trained on multicultural competency and diversity. This training should include issues dealing with culture, religion, family types, and White privilege. Teachers can also have images that all the children in the class could relate to. To ensure that the students are able to work with and possibly become friends with others who may be different from them, teachers can purposely arrange the seating so that children of different backgrounds have to work and talk to each other. One piece of advice that could make this process easy is for teachers to teach their students as they would like other teachers to teach their own children—with care, kindness, enthusiasm, patience, and the will to inspire.

I would ask teachers to treat the biracial student like any other student in the class. To make the biracial student feel included and validated, teachers can have multiracial and multicultural literature available. Teachers can celebrate differences through activities and cultural celebrations.

If students come to class with a behavior, academic, or emotional problem, teachers should not assume it is due to their racial background.

Wil Parker, African American
Regional Outreach Director, National Board for Professional
** Teaching Standards**
Washington, DC

We need to raise the level of excellence so that race is not an indicator of success or failure. I suggest the following:

- *Teachers need to use race as an enabler, not as an inhibitor. For example, Black urban kids—Black kids show up black; they have no other way to show up, and urban is just where they live. Teachers need to find out why the child learns like that.*
- *Teachers need to find out what they value about race. What do they value about being instructional leaders?*
- *Teachers need to take a deep look at their bias. They need to ask themselves, "Why do I have that bias?" It's okay to have the bias, but they can't use it to determine whether a child will be successful or not.*
- *Teachers have to look through a new lens. They have to understand the relevance of the students' values.*
- *Good instructional leaders have to want to have those conversations about race that make them uncomfortable because we must find out what others hold as their values.*
- *Teachers must ask themselves, "How do we use that to create relevance to excellence in what we are teaching?"*

Karen Notarainni, White
Mother of a Mixed-Identity Child
Houston, Texas

What I'd like teachers to know about ethnicity and race is that it needs to be an open conversation on an on-going basis; political correctness that requires a moratorium on the subject of race is not working. (On the other hand, I don't trust enough teachers to be open-minded enough to discuss it without trampling over students' feelings and developing self-esteem.)

The school curriculum should include more examples of achievements by more diverse people, and not just during Martin Luther King, Jr. week.

Charlane Pralle-Janssen, White
Principal/Curriculum Director
Hampton, Iowa

We have to promote our differences and understand each other, no matter what we do. We have to understand the Hispanic culture of the people in my town; we don't need to tromp on each other; we need to take the best to become a different picture, to find the beauty. When I paint, I blend many colors to make something more beautiful; that's what it's all about—different times—we have to get used to it. I grew up a blue-eyed white girl in a world of color—there are lots of types of beauty that are not about the blue eyes and blonde hair.

In our district, we have tried the following:

1. *Use a Circle of Friends: purposely put other people around the child to spend time with him or her.*

2. *Use one-on-one counseling for all students, especially at middle school.*

3. *Understand issues of poverty. Don't mistake issues of poverty for race.*

4. *Expose children to career programs.*

5. *Bring in foods and the histories of other cultures. Because we are in rural Iowa, sometimes we have to intentionally bring in experiences that students would not have the opportunity to experience.*

6. *Plan activities with the larger communities so that students can share likes and differences with others.*

7. *Create a panel of your parents and students of different ethnicities and have them present to teachers.*

8. *Work to create trust with communities of color. Purposely put interpreters and parents on district planning committees.*

9. *Post art and posters with visuals of all kinds of people throughout the schools. We have one that says, "We're all different; we have become not a melting pot, but a beautiful mosaic."*

Diana Breckenridge, Biracial
Optometrist
Los Angeles, California

When teachers have an open, inviting way, I find that I trust them with information about being mixed if they're interested in knowing about my background. If they're really strict and don't show any liking for me, it's harder to warm up. I can tell if they like me by their body language. This body language includes expressive eyebrows, lots of facial expression, a smile, a gentle demeanor, someone who may sit down at eye level with their hands folded gently in front of their body versus behind. To me, hands folded behind are a sign of insecurity in performing their instruction.

Teachers can improve their instruction by calling on each child, not just the few who "think like you." They can balance out attention for each person. A lot of children hate to speak in class, but that's the only way to give them their attention and get them to communicate.

Also, instead of just having one child speak at a time, teachers can use a call and response where children respond in unison; that eases the tension.

Teachers should not cause the child embarrassment by asking questions in front of a whole class about some curiosity about ethnicity. This is not something a mixed child wants to do—be singled out in front of the class.

Chelsea Breckenridge, Mixed—Black/White
High School Student
Laguna Beach, California

I think some teachers don't realize this: Try to be careful what you say. You never know when someone might be a different race, and you might be insulting him or her.

Glynnis Breckenridge, White
Teacher and Mother of Biracial Children—Hispanic/Black/White
Laguna Beach, California

I would suggest simple things such as wearing ethnic jewelry once in a while, saying positive things about other cultures, and being very careful not to say anything negative—to try to look at the world as one whole place that is a home to everyone.

Some teachers are so quick to make that judgment call and to treat that child a certain way. You think it would be the opposite, but it has been so prevalent in my experience. I have been PTO president, room mother, and so on. I would tell teachers to try to refrain from making that judgment call.

Also, realize that ethnic kids and mixed kids are very likely to have low self-esteem. The mixed child may not have a choice of what group they belong to—the whites not liking the black in her; and the blacks thinking she is high yellow, so she may find herself an outcast.

For kindergarten and preschool teachers, put up pictures of all different colors of skin in artwork and mention how beautiful all the skin colors are. Ask students about the different colors of people they have seen. Have the kids draw a picture.

Stan Breckenridge, PhD, African American
College Professor, Father of Biracial Children
Laguna Beach, California

Elementary school teachers should know not to make a choice for a child regarding the child's ethnicity or race. Don't assume how the child identifies herself or whom she wants to associate with in the classroom. Teachers should realize that young people are experiencing different levels of cultural association.

Teachers need to know what it means to be white. The notion of biracial and multiculturalism are different; don't try to force kids to think that when you speak about multiculturalism, you are meeting the needs of biracial kids. Multiculturalism is when you are talking about things; biracial means you are talking about people. Multiculturalism has something to do with other cultures' traditions; biracialism is talking about people, the person part.

When we deal with biracial, it has to do with the visual. Some assume it has to do with the bloodline, but it is more with what you see.

A teacher should be cognizant of the terminology, past and present, that relates to cultural differences, for example, handkerchief head, *referring to an* Uncle Tom. *A teacher has to be very aware of those derogatory and pejorative terms so they know how to speak to a child who uses them or to the child they were directed towards.*

The elementary student may be trying to pass if they can. My son's hair enabled him to pass at a younger age; my daughter's hair was not typically white, so it was harder for her to pass.

Francesca Maria Apodaca, Chicana/White/African American
Receptionist, Mother of Mixed Children
New Mexico

The most important thing is to take your cues from the child. Just because someone is from a certain ethnicity and looks a certain way, don't assume they have information about a certain culture or belong to a certain culture. Take what information your students give you and use that as a reference point. Instead of asking, "How is that possible?" or thinking, "He doesn't look anything like that," have an open mind and treat your students who look different the same as you treat everyone else.

April Warren Grice, African American
Doctoral Student in Social Justice
Champaign, Illinois

Oftentimes students with multiracial backgrounds are pigeonholed into one category or another, and because educators try so desperately to place them in stereotypical boxes, students are shortchanged on their educational journey. By educators trying to make students choose a racial category, or even worse, picking one for them, it creates tension between the teacher and student. According to "Diversity Before Equity: Three Faculty Members Argue for a Greater Inclusiveness" found at http://www.tc.columbia.edu/news/article.htm? id=5480, this tension, which can also be seen as microaggressions, "the everyday dismissive snubs toward minorities 'often performed unconsciously'. . . negatively impact race relations." Though intentional or not, subtle nuances and remarks harm the learning environment and the learning process, which frequently wounds a student's self-confidence and contributes to indelible damage. Students need to be validated and their confidence nurtured. Therefore, it is imperative that educators recognize that different *is not* deficient *and teachers should celebrate the entire multiracial student.*

Michael Tapp, Biracial
Elementary School Teacher
Omaha, Nebraska

I do have hope for the future, and it lies in the hands of our children. I teach fourth grade. A couple of months ago, we were having a discussion about civil rights in the 1960s. Most of my students had no concept of why blacks and whites were separated. They could not comprehend why black people had to drink out of separate fountains, use separate restrooms, and eat at separate restaurants. It made no sense to them why blacks and whites had to be separate. Some of them know I am biracial, so they would ask me questions such as what would have happened to me back then, or if I would have been lynched, and so on. The fact that they very naturally asked these questions rather than responding with, "I didn't know you were black," "What does your dad look like?" "You don't look black," was very refreshing. It is very encouraging to me to see that our young people are becoming more focused on togetherness and our similarities than dwelling on our differences.

I learned a lot from that discussion, which will help me in my future endeavors as an educator. I will let kids speak openly and honestly about race. I will not encourage or persuade them to think one thing or another, they will discover their own feelings and beliefs in regard to race. I will allow them to become comfortable talking about race so they can learn to discuss it honestly and without feelings of guilt and with the hope that they will do the same thing as an adult. So many of us as adults are so uncomfortable talking about race, so afraid of offending someone or being called a racist, that it becomes counterproductive. Instead of discussing our beliefs with people of other races, we shy away from it and instead change the subject.

Tahnee Markussen, Biracial
Education Director
Omaha, Nebraska

Kids are pretty smart. If someone is full of crap, they can detect it. Teachers need to be themselves, know who they are. They need to understand their own life story. They need not impose their idea of what a multiracial child should be on the class as a whole.

Edith Beard Brady, Mixed Race: Japanese/Scotch Irish
Publisher
San Francisco, California

A teacher should have the sensitivity and awareness of the cultural richness mixed race brings to the classroom. For example, one of my teachers had been to Kenya so she knew about Kenya. The father of one of the only black students in our class was from Kenya. The teacher did a slide show and represented his father's country in a very positive light. That made him love her and feel at ease and feel valued.

Kay Cornell, White
Retired Assistant Superintendent for Instruction
Education Consultant and Coach in High Priority Schools
Detroit, Michigan

So what is it I know about race, you wonder? I grew up in a traditional, middle-class white family in Detroit, Michigan, where my only exposure to people of color was a cleaning woman—I asked her why her hands were dirty. My parents had strong prejudices, and they made certain that we lived far apart from the bad *parts of Detroit. I then spent my entire educational career in a white, middle-class suburb of Detroit. Yet somehow I became a champion of civil rights, perhaps a reaction to my family because somewhere in my heart I always knew they were wrong. Throughout my career, I have continually seen people—consciously or unconsciously—show their prejudices and fears. Ours was one of the first school districts to allow schools of choice students to attend our schools. Primarily, the students who came were students of color, mostly black. I immediately began to hear how* those students *were causing problems, didn't know how to behave, were bringing down test scores, and so on. Of course that wasn't true, but even when I showed teachers the data to prove they were wrong, they continued to spout the negatives. Those children were clearly treated differently than* our own neighborhood kids—*something unconscionable to me to this day. When I retired from the K–12 district, I began working as a coach in highly qualified schools, working with principals and teachers to improve student achievement and narrow the achievement gap. These students are primarily black, and most are children of generational poverty. One would hope that the passion and hopes for students in these schools would be different than they were in the middle-class schools. However, after five years of doing this work, I am horrified and saddened by what I see: expectations are lower, many false assumptions are made about the students and their parents, and teachers have just given up. They so often believe the following:*

1. *The students can't or won't learn.*

2. *Families don't support schools at home.*

3. *Families don't teach their children how to behave.*

4. *Families don't have high expectations for their children.*

And on and on and on. It has become clear to me that many teachers—most of whom are white and/or middle class—don't understand their students and their students' culture. I have great empathy for parents and caregivers who I believe are stretched as far as they can be—working two or three jobs, worrying about gas and food prices, and wondering sometimes how to get from day to day. The teachers don't seem to reach out to the parents to build relationships, to build bridges on which to work together. I'm not sure what will improve this situation. I can only say the following to teachers:

1. *The expectations should be as high for these children as they are for the teachers' own children. No one rises to low expectations.*

2. *Keep a positive attitude toward every child—even those most difficult to love.*

3. *Believe that parents care deeply about their children—don't assume they don't just because they don't join PTA or volunteer in the classrooms.*

4. *Stop comparing this school and these children to your children and your children's schools. These are not your children, and this is not your child's school.*

5. *Work to recognize your own biases and prejudices.*

6. *If the students don't learn from the way you're used to teaching, change your teaching methods. Don't wait for the children to change. They're doing the best they can.*

7. *Make sure your classroom reflects students' cultures. Culturally proficient teachers can create culturally proficient classrooms.*

8. *These children have a future, and they are our future. Don't ever give up on them, or they will give up on themselves. As human beings and as a nation, we can't afford that.*

My advice seems simple, yet if we are to give children of color the opportunities they deserve and want, we must change our schools, and that begins with changing ourselves.

Jennifer Duncan, Biracial
Toronto, Canada

My suggestions for teachers who are trying to understand their biracial or multiracial students (although I would find this useful for students of any racial identity) and also trying to improve their instruction are as follows:

1. *Be sensitive and open to how the students themselves identify and listen carefully for the way in which they came to this understanding of themselves. Their idea of themselves is the most important thing to be aware of in order to have a positive and effective teacher/student relationship.*

2. *Create activities that involve exploring and sharing how students see themselves (and their racial identity) with their peers. These activities will likely encourage students to embrace diversity and learn the importance of the identity others perceive you to be (e.g., black, white, biracial) versus how you see yourself. Ultimately, the peers would respect the way a student sees him or herself and realize that this is the best way to relate to that person. I cannot recount how many times I have had to correct another person's assumption or idea of what I am so that they know how I see myself and how I want others to see and understand me.*

3. *The exploration of cultural relativity is also crucial in creating an inclusive and open learning environment. A biracial person such as myself who grew up in Barbados might be considered (and consider herself) as* white, *but in the United States, that same person might be seen as* biracial *or* black. *Cultural relativity is a very important notion for teachers to understand! I would also discourage the use of "What are you?" and instead encourage students to allow their peers to describe themselves the way they want and when they want.*

4. *Explore (through a few activities or lessons) the idea of identity politics and identity formation. Speaking from my own personal experience, allow the students to explore who they are through the work that they do (incorporate the cultural diversity and contributions to U.S. history for example; research notable people from a variety of places that have impacted their lives; expand geography lessons to a global context and understand the forming of nations—many times imposed under colonialism with problematic and false borders).*

5. *Lastly, acknowledge and discuss the ever-changing nature of identity. I am a Black woman. My mother is White, and we both understand that where I am now in my life has led me to identify the way I do (what I study, who I am friends with, etc). I am always sure to be open about my privilege as a light-skinned black woman or a biracial woman in a white supremacist society, and I think this is also an important idea to teach—the acknowledgment of different forms of privilege and disadvantage that we all have.*

Curtis Linton, White
Coauthor of *Courageous Conversations About Race*
School Improvement Network
Salt Lake City, Utah

The teacher should not arm him or herself before the student arrives. Rather, the teacher should prepare to know how to respond when something is observed. It is like defensive driving—you don't drive assuming the car in front of you is going to swerve or slam on its brakes, but you are prepared in case it does.

This chapter gives advice on some of those "defensive driving" strategies (that Curtis Linton refers to above) that teachers can use to drive instruction and learning in the classroom. Most of the strategies relate to the *affective* rather than the *cognitive* since mixed-identity students are not really wired differently from any other students and learn cognitively in as many different ways as other students do. In addition to classroom strategies, there are numerous suggestions to build an inclusive racial climate where all students of color are challenged academically and accepted as part of the community with the same high expectations teachers bestow to white students. In other words, these are suggestions to build your racial literacy and cultural proficiency.

FURTHER SUGGESTIONS FOR BUILDING RACIAL LITERACY AND CULTURAL PROFICIENCY

- Be open to conversations about race.
- Include more examples of the accomplishments of diverse people in the curriculum.
- Emphasize the individuality of each student. Get to know each student as a unique individual.
- Monitor what you say.

- Study and learn about body language. Pay close attention to your body language.
- Emphasize your belief in your teaching ability to your students. This tells them they are worthy of having an excellent teacher.
- Hold high expectations for all students.
- Teach students your *hidden rules* (classroom expectations). Don't assume they know what you expect.
- Call on students equitably during instruction.
- Consider using choral responses during instruction.
- Do not single mixed-identity children out in front of their peers to ask questions about their ethnicity.
- Say positive things about other cultures and show your interest by displaying artifacts from other cultures.
- Don't prejudge students; get to know them.
- Don't assume you know what peer group the student belongs in.
- Celebrate skin colors by posting pictures of all different colors of skin in artwork; talk about how beautiful all skin colors are.
- Don't decide the race or ethnicity for a child. (Many of those interviewed shared how a teacher had forced them to choose a race they did not want to choose to mark before a test.) This can raise stress and cause the child to perform less well.
- Continue to learn about White culture and how it impacts your instruction.
- Do not segregate students in any way.
- Hold high expectations for every student. Do not feel sorry for students of color.
- Learn the terms your students use. If you don't know what they mean, ask the students. Ask them to make a dictionary for you.
- Be aware that students may be weaving in and out of identities. Do not identify for a student.
- Include multiracial and multicultural literature in the curriculum.
- Celebrate difference through activities and cultural celebrations.
- Do not assume a problem that a mixed student has is due to his or her racial background—it usually is not.
- Continue learning about multicultural competency and diversity. This training should include issues dealing with culture, religion, family types, and White privilege.
- Arrange desks so that children of different backgrounds have to work and talk to each other.
- Avoid assuming that the child will identify with just his or her minority culture or with any identity for that matter.
- Allow for honest conversations about race. Set conditions for conversation (see *Courageous Conversations About Race*) and do not shut it down.
- Teach the truth about white privilege, what it is, and how it affects society.
- Avoid stereotyping. Understand that we will never know how another feels but that we can always empathize.
- Create support groups for students.
- Use poetry to jumpstart classroom discussions about culture. Poems are available on the Internet.
- Encourage students to express themselves. Art in its many forms gives children a way to vent their inner turmoil.

- Have students investigate different cultures through class projects.
- Incorporate cultural richness into the curriculum.
- Start a professional learning community (PLC) centered around cultural proficiency.
- Incorporate cultural richness into the curriculum.
- Start a professional learning community (PLC) centered around cultural proficiency.
- Start a 20-minute Friday coffee group before school to discuss ways to improve instruction and relate to students.
- Invite a colleague in to observe your teaching. Ask your colleague to observe you for the strategy you commit to implementing.
- Keep a journal about your journey of cultural proficiency. Keep track of what strategies you implement and the results you find in the classroom.
- Commit to reading one book each quarter from the list of suggested resources. Share and discuss with colleagues.

You've heard from those interviewed for the book, and you found additional strategies listed throughout the book. The *Call to Action* is a request to you.

Decide which strategies work for you and begin with small steps by committing to implementing one to three strategies. Which one to three strategies will you commit to implement?

_____

_____

_____

_____

It is very exciting to include suggestions from individuals who have lived their lives in families with mixed-identity children or who are mixed themselves. It is clear that the very populations we seek to understand have much to say to us if we create space for their talk and then quietly listen. This book is an attempt to create space and listen. I am deeply grateful to all who contributed their thoughts so that we may continue our journeys as educators. In Chapter 10, we hear the voices of the future, young people who want to share their stories with you.

SUGGESTED READING MATERIAL

Gay, G. (2000). *Culturally responsive teaching: Theory, research, and practice.* NY: Teachers College Press.

Henze, R., Norte, E., Sather, S. E., & Walker, E. (2002). *Leading for diversity: How school leaders promote interethnic relations.* Thousand Oaks, CA: Corwin.

Lindsey, R. (2005). *The culturally proficient school: An implementation guide for school leaders.* Thousand Oaks, CA: Corwin.

Pollock, M. (2008). *Everyday antiracism: Getting real about race in school.* NY: The New Press.

Robins, N. K., Lindsey, R. B., Lindsey, D. B., & Terrell, R. (2002). *Culturally proficient instruction: A guide for people who teach.* Thousand Oaks, CA: Corwin.

Schreck, M. K. (2009). *Transformers: Creative teachers for the 21st century.* Thousand Oaks, CA: Corwin.

10

Future Voices

My identity might begin with the fact of my race, but it didn't, couldn't end there. At least that's what I would choose to believe.

—President Barack Obama

In this final chapter, our journey brings us to the voices of today's students and recent college graduates. Their stories are presented in an uninterrupted format with reflective prompts at the end of the chapter.

Alicia Notarainni, Brazilian, Born 1996
Elementary School Student, Houston, Texas
Karen Notarainni's Daughter
Written narrative

In my learning center *at school that consists of four classes of 25 students each at school, there are only about six black and Asian kids, and I am greatly outraged at this because I know there should be more diversity than that! At my old school in California, there were a lot of diverse kids. I had one white friend and one black, for pickle's sake!! There were that many!! And I know that it is not a place like Florida, where there are a lot, but it should be more diverse than that. Seriously!!!*

I'm uncomfortable about comparing white and black. The closest thing I am is black. On forms, I identify myself as black *because I'm not Asian, White, or Hispanic. I'm proud to be Brazilian, but I can't tell people that on forms because there isn't a place to tell that. It's either* white *or* black.

I was proud to not be white because it was so common. Race has nothing to do with understanding the whole person unless your personal thoughts are thinking that one is superior to the other. I know I'm adopted, and I know that I'm not a part of both of my parents. I just wish that I would stop thinking that people are treating me like I'm different because I look black. It would be easier to be fully black because it would be something to be proud of—different than white.

I think it would be easier if they had all the categories there are so you could be specific and not have all those troubles with choosing. I am very proud of being Brazilian because it is not white, so that I have more to explain to people and help them get to know me. If I were white, or if everyone were white, life would be boring with no small differences to talk about or notice in other people. I could be calmer with diversity because I would know that I was not different. It wouldn't be all white people to look at me as though I were different.

I am different from white people because of my hair and my skin, mostly. That is all people pay attention to when they think that I am black. There isn't anything else to see about me. They may see that I have other characteristics that define me from them, but they do not have anything to do with the fact that I look black. That is important because if people think that I look black, I am uncomfortable because I feel that they think I am black, and I don't fit in.

I feel that I am different when I am with white people because, obviously, I am not like them. But when I am with a group or at a place with diversity, I feel as if I fit in, and being a person of different color is not an issue.

Chris Lent, Mixed, Born 1992
High School Student, St. Louis, Missouri
Written narrative

I'm very intelligent, and I love to read and write and work beyond college level on both. On the forms, I mark Caucasian. *I define myself as mixed since that's what I am. But when I walk out the door, I don't think of myself as white, black, or even mixed. I see myself as me—and me alone. Race doesn't limit me to what I can do.*

To me, choosing one racial heritage over another is just stupid. Even if you didn't have a choice, you should be proud of your racial heritage, whether it be white, black, or any other mix. I'm not the kind of guy to discriminate. If I enjoy being around you, then I'll be around you more. Race doesn't mean a thing to me when it comes to relationships with other people. I decide my own identification; no one else does it for me.

If I'm asked, "What are you?" I tell them I'm mixed. It really doesn't affect me in any way. It doesn't bother me. If they're curious, then I'll answer them. My advice is to just ask them. A lot of people like me will just answer you straight ahead. I assert my mixed-race identity in my personality, the music I listen to, and the way I dress. My curly hair gives it away. Also, the way I dress shows people I act more white *than* black.

I've never really felt that I'm an outsider because of my race. I can fit into any group of people. Race doesn't matter to me. When I went through my skater/reb *phase, I was usually made fun of because I'm biracial. Sometimes, they would bring up the subject of parents, and a lot of the time, I was the center of attention.*

As long as teachers are good teachers, they can teach any student. Teachers should avoid pointing out biracial and multiracial students, and they shouldn't be biased against children of biracial and multiracial heritage.

Chelsea Breckenridge, Mixed, Born 1993
Student, Laguna Beach, California
Stan and Glynnis Breckenridge's Daughter
Transcribed face-to-face interview

I'm the youngest out of five kids, and I'm African American, but the perfect category for me is mixed because I'm neither all-black nor all-white. I'm both.

I never had different development stages of race that I went through. I was always just one thing. It never really changed. I have more facial things and physical features of African Americans: my hair is curly and wavy and has an African American coarse texture; my legs are different, not skinny; my eyes, maybe they look exotic. Mom says, but I don't notice it.

Racial things happen once in a while. There is a Hispanic girl with light-skin tone and a Hispanic accent at our high school, and in our science lab groups, kids were teasing her, saying, "Go back to the border." I was with two of my friends. The only way my friends think of Black people is that they are from the ghetto, so when one of my friends tried to sound Black, my other friend said, "She sounds blacker than you." One of my friends was going in a new car to east Los Angeles, and another friend told her she would get shot. There is an interesting lady who always walks around our block. After the fires occurred in the area, she said to my dad one day, "Did you start those fires?" We don't know her that well. She said, "We're watching you," as she walked by me in the garden. I have some sympathy for people like her because they think they are the only people that exist in the world and that African American people are always doing something wrong, and we're up to no good. She could have said worse, not that I don't get bothered by it. That's just the way the world is sometimes. I feel kind of special because I get to be mixed with both black and white so I feel kind of special that way. I've never felt separated from others, just more insulted sometimes. I've been going to our church since I was two, and I've known everyone since then, and I can still say hi to everyone—church is my second home.

I want to become a teacher.

Alex Hudgens, Biracial, Born 1990
Student, Webster Groves High School
Webster Groves, Missouri

I am currently a senior in high school. I'm a varsity cheerleader and a drum major in the marching band. I play the baritone saxophone in jazz band and Wind Symphony. I'm a pole-vaulter and a 400-meter runner for the track team. I'm the vice-president of Distributive Education Clubs of America (DECA) at my high school because I love business. I'm a member of many other groups at my high school, I volunteer a bunch, and I often represent my high school at events that call for student representatives. I'm EXTREMELY busy because of all of this, but I figure that there will never be another time in my life when I'll get to participate in all that I do—I'm living it up while I can. I'm a very active member of my church youth group, and my faith is one of the most important aspects of my life. I love playing the piano (for the past 12 years), photography, exercise, and trying new things. I feel most satisfied when I'm serving people, especially on mission trips. I'm going to college next year to study something along the lines of communications, public relations, and psychology. I'm very interested in broadcast journalism—I WILL be an anchor on the Today Show *someday. I'm a determined, genuine, enthusiastic person who loves to meet new people. Finally, my favorite color is gray!*

I always mark the biracial box on forms if it is an option. I choose to not define myself as Caucasian *or* African American *because I think that I have aspects of both cultures in my genetic makeup and personality. I believe that most individuals develop racial and ethnic identities based upon the environment in which they're brought up. Regardless of the color of your skin, you're probably going to base your beliefs, behaviors, clothing, eating habits, and such on whatever you've known your whole life.*

I have been blessed with a life where people don't usually place me under any specific racial category, and I don't label myself either. I'm just Alex.

I have been able to use my ethnicity to truly reach out to different groups of people. Since racism does still exist, and social stigmas and stereotypes are prevalent in our high schools, people seem to respond well to someone successful and caring who comes from a mixed background. I'm a people-person by nature, and I've found that my race background often presents opportunities to interact with people that I might not have had otherwise.

I have been asked, "What are you?" at least a million times! I usually reply with something such as, "I'm biracial," because I'm not particularly a fan of the term mixed. *I'm not offended when others use mixed to classify someone, but it isn't entirely respectful in my opinion. You can have mixed fruits and mixed vegetables, but do we really need to classify people that way? After telling people that I'm biracial, they usually proceed into guessing what my background is instead of just asking. Though I'm simply black and white, people never guess correctly; it's always, "Mexican and Chinese?" or "Indian and somewhere in Latin America?" There's typically some Asian country thrown into the mix because my eyes are almond shaped, but my hair is dark brown with red streaks, so that throws people off. The most frequently used term to describe my look is exotic, which basically translates into, "I have no idea what you are." I'm never offended when people ask me this question. If asked, "what are you?" I would probably say something such as, "a girl, a cheerleader," or so on, just out of spite. My race doesn't constitute what I am. Honestly, I find it entertaining to watch people try and guess what my ethnicity is, especially because hardly anyone guesses correctly.*

I think that others place an exaggerated emphasis on my physical appearance due to me being biracial. I don't really enjoy recognition, but I get told that I'm pretty a lot. It isn't that I enjoy being pretty or being told that I'm pretty; I just like the fact that my physical features are kind of unclassifiable and unique. It's nice to be an individual and really look like an individual since the mixing of my parents' races make someone who looks different than everyone else. Plus, the year-round tan is always a plus!

I think that my biraciality affects others around me because it exposes people to a type of culture that they may not have ever been introduced to before. I've had friends who have had to defend me because they happen to be white when someone makes a racist comment about me being a black girl. I think that my race potentially threatens others because people are threatened by what they don't know and what they cannot classify.

I think that females experience a bit more difficulty regarding issues of race when it comes to romantic relationships. I've noticed that when dating, multiracial women often only choose to date one race of men. It seems that if you're black and white, you have to choose whether you date black men or white men. I've observed that apparently, it can't be both ways. I believe that people should date whomever they want regardless of race or any other social standards.

I would tell teachers not to treat us as if we're a different species. I think that instruction of students depends totally on the personality of that student; just be sure not to treat students differently because you don't know how to respond to their race. We don't need teachers adding to any tension that racism in our schools might present. I would say to teachers: Love your job or don't do it. Prove to your students that you truly care about their individual success and that you're passionate about your area of expertise through everything that you do.

For biracial or multiracial students specifically: Use these students' ethnicity to your advantage. Encourage them to embrace their racial identity and explore every part of their background. They can also really be a light to different groups of students if encouraged to strive to reach their full potential.

Bassam Khawaja, Multiracial, Born 1989
College Student, St. Paul, Minnesota
Written narrative

I was born in 1989 in Ithaca, New York, to a Palestinian father and a Polish American mother. My father could not be there as he was under collective punishment in the West Bank and was forbidden from leaving. Since then, I've lived in New York, the West Bank, Norway, Lebanon, and Minnesota. I am a musician, an athlete, a student, and an activist. But through none of this have I ever felt any sense of belonging based on my race. To be multiracial is to experience the feelings of an outsider no matter where you are, who you are with, or what you are doing. In the United States, I am given uncomfortable looks when people learn I am here from the Middle East. In Lebanon, I've been attacked for speaking English on the street. I can only fit in by choosing to embody half of my identity, by playing a role that I can accept and be comfortable with. And while this is in no way an assumed identity, it is only a part of my identity, as I am rarely allowed to be both halves at once.

Being multiracial means having no preformed racial identity to fall back on. And while this can weaken your initial sense of self, it means that there is an intelligent process involved with forming your own identity. You are forced to think actively rather than simply take on the homogeneous identity of your ancestors; that is something you simply don't have. Because of this, you approach issues of race very differently. It is impossible to otherize, and thus dehumanize, members of another race, because you yourself belong to multiple races. The easy way out that makes cross-racial understanding and interaction so difficult in today's society simply ceases to exist. Being multiracial has both positive and negative factors on the life and experiences of the individual. Growing up without a solid sense of identity and belonging is difficult and confusing. But at the same time, it forces you to think more actively and allows you to experience multiple identities.

For teachers:

There is no single straightforward piece of advice that I could offer to teachers because I deeply believe, possibly because of my multiracial sense of self, that we are people first and foremost. We live in a society that is deeply embedded in racism, where it is extremely easy for people to think of one another simply along dividing lines, but that is not an excuse to make any assumptions about students based on their racial identity. Just like students of any race, a multiracial student will have had certain experiences growing up that will be a part of his or her identity. That does not mean that they need to be treated a certain way because of this. The only thing one can do is to make no assumptions about the identity of the student and the extent to which the issue of race plays in to that identity.

Christina Amalia Andrade, White/Latina, Born 1990
College Student, University of Missouri/Columbia
Telephone interview

In quite a lot of ways, I grew up as a typical white suburban kid; I never really saw anything different about myself. My family speaks Spanish at family reunions, and I have two grandmothers who cook different food.

I had a couple of recent experiences in college. One was in an education class of predominantly white students that actually dealt mostly with race at schools. My group ironically had to do a presentation on Mexican Latino culture. That was an awkward moment because no one knew I was Latina, so we got up and talked about it, and there was a real disconnect.

There is a set of cultural expectations for Latino students. The way teachers see them is that they expect the boys are going to be rowdy, and the girls won't pay attention; they allow Spanish students to hide behind language; 90% are bilingual; others pick up English fairly quickly. They will speak in Spanish about you, but I wish more teachers would call them out on it.

I started substitute teaching in a suburb in St. Louis, and I was working in a kindergarten class with maybe 40% to 50% white students, 30% African American students, and 20% Hispanic students. I asked the kids to come to attention in Spanish. When teachers take the time to cross that language barrier, it really means something.

Physical appearance doesn't identify as any ethnicity. There has been a false assumption that I was Jewish. My one brother and I are much darker and have coarse hair, and my other brother is very pale. I know my parents had some adjustments, getting used to each other and family. My mother's parents weren't accepting of my dad at first. There is definitely a language barrier between mother and her mother-in-law.

I suggest teachers do the following: make an attempt to learn the language, approach the students, and ask how they as a teacher can support them. Connect lessons to the kids in class. I had a chip on my shoulder about that because my ethnic literature experience was not varied. Why not use a piece of literature by Sandra Cisneros? Holden Caulfield is a character that speaks strongly to teen males; even today that's their favorite book, but I haven't had a single experience like that.

Understand the audience you're teaching to and tailor your content to that. Bring in short pieces; give everyone something different to talk about. Even if there are no Hispanic kids in class, using Hispanic literature is a valuable perspective to give to other students. High school students are the center of their own world; bringing in multicultural fiction and asking questions, such as, "What would that be like?" and "Is that like something I'm doing now?" are important for students. It allows them to step outside of themselves, and I think that's very valuable and gives a perspective.

Taylor Donaven Crask, Mixed, Born 1990
High School Student, St. Louis, Missouri
Telephone interview

I am mixed; my mother is white and my dad is black. I plan to go to Forest Park Community College to study culinary arts. I consider myself a white person mostly. I don't live with my father; I live in a predominantly white neighborhood. Others see me as mostly white or mixed. I assert my mixed identity only when it helps me.

I hang with all kinds of guys. I don't get hassled. If you saw me, you'd know why. I'm 310 pounds, 6'1". I like to make people laugh, and I try to be different. My nickname is Gumbie.

I never feel that I can't hang out with anyone I want. Being mixed just doesn't matter; I never have a feeling that I can't hang out with anyone I want. I have a good friend selection; if someone would feel I couldn't hang with them, then those friends come and go. I'm a happy guy. I'm just another kid, and I'm really outgoing. I can turn anything into a positive.

Young people ignore race more; it's not a big deal; we can hang out with anyone; but segregation is still strong in our school. The lunchroom has Mexican tables, Black tables, and White tables, so it is still strong—you also don't see white kids playing at basketball hoops.

They can tell I'm mixed, I have black *people hair, and I have freckles.*

I was always a big guy. I was always funny, big, outgoing.

It's harder for girls; girls judge more than guys. If you have nappy *hair, you can't hang out with the white girls. It's stupid.*

I'd tell teachers to treat everyone the same. Just TEACH.

Ashley Meyer, Mixed, Black/White, Born 1992
Graig Meyer's daughter, High School Student, North Carolina
Telephone interview

I don't think race has an extreme impact; I'm accepted in groups like the black and white groups; I think it's interesting; you're half white, but when you hang out with black friends, you have the best of both worlds. I'm comfortable with both.

I usually get from my white friends, "Why do you act so white?" but with my black friends, it doesn't bother them at all the way I act.

Well, even today I was with some of my friends, they always say, "Oh, your mom is white." Both of my parents are white. So many think my parents are black. I just tell them, "Those are my parents." Sometimes I tell them I'm adopted, and sometimes I just leave it at that.

A lot of experiences that are memorable are the things people say to me, like they'll say, "Oh, you are part black, but your hair is this way." People have different questions. I have insight into what other people are seeing when they ask questions about me. I'm comfortable with my family and, I don't see them differently. I don't see my parents as white and me as biracial. I just see them as one family. I have biracial and multiracial friends—some are different. One friend is black and Mexican and mixed with white or black. We just happen to be friends. I have lots of different friends.

My generation—we're aware of race, but I think we're coming to a point where we just accept it; we may make comments, but we're very accepting of each other and other races; we've grown up surrounded with people of different colors, ideas, opinions. We're comfortable with what we've been around, and we're more accepting of it.

My racial identity began when at one point in seventh grade I realized I had more white friends, and I did not feel accepted, so I had to find a way to be accepted by people—I made friends with blacks and became more comfortable with the black American part of me.

What are you? I'm black or I'm mixed with black and white.

About my teachers: I don't notice any different treatment from teachers; my advice would be to treat multiracial students how you would treat any other students. There is really nothing my teachers need to change.

Mani Barajas-Alexander, African American/Mexican, Born 1986
Recent College Graduate, Tennis Professional
Telephone interview

My dad is African American and was born in Philadelphia. My mom was born in McAllen, Texas, and grew up in part in Houston. She is second-generation Mexican American. I am half African American and half Mexican. I used to speak Spanish, but lost it. I understand a good bit but can't speak it very well. It is something I am working on.

I attended public schools first through eighth grades then went to a private Catholic high school. It was pretty conservative, and everyone definitely learned.

Out of the nonathletes, 95% of the student population was white; the football, basketball, and track student athletes were predominantly black or some other minority. I played tennis in high school and college and graduated from Longwood University where I was captain of the tennis team and played in the Division I program. I was a business major with a marketing concentration and was very active on campus the last two years; I founded two organizations, one of which became an official part of the business school, and the other was the tennis program. I was also an active member of the student advisory committee.

It's interesting because I don't fit the typical stereotypes of a black person or a Mexican, and there's a little bit of pride that I'm that combination. What do you think I am? When I ask people, they always answer half white, half black; half white, half something. Maybe only two people have guessed what I am. When I'm with my Mexican side of the family, I look like them, and when I'm with my black side of my family, I look like them. Maybe because of the way I talk and dress, but I feel I'm more accepted and have an easier time with white people. I went to Martha's Vineyard in the summer to a community that has many black middle- and upper-income people. I had no problem fitting in, but around here, it's hard to find things in common with minorities in the area. It is not necessarily a race issue; it's more a class issue. That's my observation. I think I relate to people's backgrounds—what their values are, what their education is—not their skin color. It's much more difficult to feel accepted and closer to those who are either black or Mexican who are lower-class. I don't look down on them. I don't know how to explain it; it's hard to explain it. They feel I think I'm better than they are; I may be wearing a certain brand or speaking English, not using enough slang. That's the frustrating thing. I have friends say you don't act black; you don't dress a certain way. How are black people or white people or any group of people supposed to dress? Proper English is proper English. And then the media distorts all the images of people.

I really haven't had too many girlfriends; I've had a straightedge schedule and plans and never wanted serious commitment. I haven't had time, but of the couple I have had one was half Mexican and half Argentinian, one African American, and the last one was Romanian. I find myself attracted to Latinas and light-skinned black girls. I would feel more comfortable with people of my skin color, but at the same time I can get along with lots of different people. It's more them accepting my behavior; it's not me forcing myself on them. It depends what kind of person you are, and that goes back to values. My closest friends are international—from all over the world.

My advice to teachers:

I would say the best thing—I try to do with everybody I teach (tennis)—is to approach teaching in a variety of different ways. Everybody in class learns differently, so teachers should diversify their techniques. Do the same thing for all races and classes. Be open minded to students' personal backgrounds and what they have experienced.

Have the teacher create an environment where everybody feels comfortable because students are not going to share the truth about anything if they're not comfortable in class. The result is that other people miss out on hearing all the perspectives in the classroom, and everybody's learning suffers.

I notice race sometimes in little actions that people do say: I remember being overly sensitive to race in one situation. I was on a panel speaking to high school students at a college tennis-recruiting seminar. I was up there speaking and was 19 at the time. They asked me to give my best advice to kids. I gave a well-thought out answer, I guess, because afterward people came up and said, "Good advice." Then one guy said, "I didn't expect that from you, but great advice." I thought to myself, Did he mean I was being mature for my age or sounding good for a minority? *I think that is a very common thing that happens with multiracial people and minorities; people second guess people's actions and words. Is it race-based or human-based? Is this because I'm black and Mexican or because I'm young and inexperienced?*

I don't really use race as an excuse or anything like that. I definitely see race as an obstacle; it's like a geometry problem; it's a given; you are not going to have the upper hand; it's a motivational thing to make me work and try to excel in whatever I'm doing. I know I have to be that much better; it's like Barack Obama; he's so consistent with his message and strategy. He has the bar set so high for him; if he were white, it wouldn't be that way.

This chapter included the voices of younger people and ends with Jennifer Duncan's narrative. Jennifer is the oldest person included in this chapter of future voices. Her narrative offers a sound place to complete our journey of narratives. Read and enjoy.

Jennifer Duncan, Woman of Color, Born 1982
Recent College Graduate, Toronto, Canada
Written narrative

To understand where my writing is located, I must describe who I think I am right now. I am a 25-year-old woman of color living in Toronto (a very multicultural but still quite segregated city). My father is black, and my mother is white, but their race does not define me. I have been accepted within the black community (usually after explaining that I self-identify as first a woman of color and then a black woman) and acknowledge the fact that I am not perceived to be white, like my mother. It's not necessarily a case of not feeling accepted within the white community or the white side of my family for example. Instead, when I look in the mirror, I see a person of color, and that is a beautiful thing. I find the label person or woman of color really useful because it is an inclusive label and also a uniting one.

It is, however, interesting to note that amongst the vibrant Caribbean community in Toronto (a majority who are Jamaican), I am seen to be white *or* clear *(due to many factors—the way I speak, the way my hair is described as* nice *often meaning* white hair *or* not black hair, *my facial features). Upon spending a few months in Barbados, I was also seen as white. When I discussed this new experience with a friend there (as I had never been called white up to that point—I was in my early 20s), he explained that in a majority* black *society such as Barbados—anyone that is other is often understood or looked at as white. I loved this newfound perceived identity for one reason—it illustrates so clearly how race is relative. Note: I don't think this makes race artificial in any way though. I didn't change, but the perception others have of my race (and me) does (and usually that is dependent on whether it is a majority black society—such as the Caribbean or a majority white society—such as Canada or the United States).*

With that said, my own ideas of who I am change constantly and will continue to change in the future. I am quite fascinated with the need for people to put me into an easy-to-understand or read category, and I reject this idea because this is not who I am. I suppose more than anything, I use my self-identification as a way to challenge rigid and one-dimensional ways of understanding people through race, gender, sexual orientation, and so on. I do think there is a preoccupation with labels in our society. I realize it is much easier to compartmentalize people into races, genders, nations, and so on, but when I really think about it, these terms rarely symbolize me. So when people ask me, "What are you?" or "Are you black, white, Indian, Chinese and every mixture in between?" I choose not to answer unless I want to (and that happens with people I am familiar and comfortable with, not strangers). I think not knowing is unsettling to many people I meet, and I often wonder why we can't begin a dialogue around race that isn't based in categories, crossing categories, or dichotomies.

I prefer to think of race as a social construction because while race, and therefore racial definitions, might not necessarily apply to some people, I think there is no doubt that race as a social construct has an impact on many people (particularly in neo colonial/western/white supremacist societies) such as myself. I see the difference between how I am treated with my black female friends and my white female friends. I notice how many men (especially black men who are brainwashed by our neo colonial society) find me attractive for my features (racial markers) that are black enough to be appealing (stereotypes of course but nonetheless—the larger butt, the curvier figure) and white enough (nice hair) to be nonoffensive to the white dominated society we live in. I know race began as something meaningless and completely constructed, but we cannot fail to acknowledge its great and real impact on our lives.

I agree with Rainier Spencer (2006) in the inadequacy of a label such as "first generation biracial person." For some reason, this reminds me a great deal of quantifying a person's race. The United States has a rich history in this (the historic terms of quadroon, octoroon), but it isn't a useful framework. When does a generation start within a family when it comes to race? I really don't think this is possible to answer without using this quantifying method (a completely useless one if you ask me). Of course, a child's identity is shaped in part by his or her understanding of what race he or she is (which is affected by, among other things, what they see their parents, the one-up generation, to be)—but I think the determining factor of any fairly accurate identity label or term would begin with that child, and so the use for first, second, third and so on generation is not needed at all.

The narratives in this chapter offer a myriad of life experiences and opportunities for discussion. Think about the narratives and consider these questions:

What common experiences do you find in the narratives?

_____

_____

_____

_____

What experiences do mixed-identity individuals share with other students of color?

_____

_____

_____

_____

Thinking back over the narratives, what did the students say that gives you hope for the future?

_____

_____

_____

_____

These young people are doing just fine. Their mixed identity is part of who they are but does not define *all* they are. They give me hope for the future at a time when the notion of *mixed race* is as obsolete as the notion of any *race* of people, a time when all educators recognize the cultural capital all children bring with them as they enter our classrooms.

Comment on the statement, "Their mixed identity is part of who they are but does not define all they are."

_____

_____

_____

_____

Join me in writing what we learned in this chapter.

_____

_____

_____

_____

11

The Journey's End and Next Steps

Describe your feelings at the end of our journey.

_____

_____

_____

_____

We've reached the end of our journey. Think about what we've done.

As we read the book and reflected, we did the following:

- Examined our assumptions, values, and beliefs about ourselves and others
- Learned from other educators, students, and parents and interacted with their narratives through written responses
- Continued to develop cultural proficiency and racial literacy

In addition, our journey provided the following:

- Definitions, histories, and complexities of race
- Opportunities to assess our knowledge and comfort levels surrounding issues of race

- Examples of the challenges students of mixed-racial identity may face that differ from your other students
- Strategies to implement in your educational setting that support multiracial students and their families

WHAT I LEARNED

- Racial categories are not biological realities.
- People don't fit neatly into racial groups.
- We are treated as racial group members and need to understand what that means and how it impacts our daily lives.
- Individuals experience race differently; there is no one racial experience.
- As a responsible educator, I need to continue my journey of racial literacy and cultural proficiency.

This journey's end feels like a beginning to me. I know there is much more to do. There are more books to read; there are more people to learn from; there are more experiences to have as I continue my journey of cultural equity and racial literacy.

When I began this book, it was long before the election of 2008. My observation from talking with others in my generation was that we shared common perceptions about issues of race. This changed dramatically when I began to interview younger people. My observation—and it is only *my* observation, and I take full responsibility for this statement—is that young people, born in 1980 or later (and this is not an exact date, for I include my son born in December, 1979), see the world quite differently. Yes, they see the world differently, and they see color differently. And it makes me feel hopeful, very hopeful. The world is changing as the election has proven, and we can change. Even though I'm aware that we must not lose sight of all the work to be done surrounding issues of race, I do believe we have new sets of eyes who envision the work differently. Together, hopefully, we will do the work necessary to make the concept of race obsolete.

With that in mind, my *Call to Action* involves the following antiracist strategies:

- Continue your journey to learn about yourself by sharing your story and taking part in *Courageous Conversations About Race*.
- Keep a journal of your equity work.
- Find colleagues to take the journey with you.
- Call attention to racism when you observe it.
- Implement educational strategies that support equity for all students.
- Be and stay hopeful. It is a new century!

This new century brought the birth of my first grandchild, and I began this book by dedicating it to her. So it is fitting to end with words about Eva from Brenda, her mother. Brenda writes,

> *I now look at the whopping eyes of my five-month-old daughter, Eva Salomé Àlvarez Davis. She is Mexican; she is Puerto Rican; she is White; and she is Black. Yet, when I look at her, I don't see any of this. All I see is a little girl who has the potential to enjoy life and to develop her own thoughts; I see a little girl who will be confident in her skin regardless of ethnic and racial backgrounds; and I see a little girl who will benefit from being multicultural and who will cross all boundaries despite color and language.*
>
> *I'm excited to be her mama.*

I'm excited to be her grandma.

Brenda and I see Eva through family eyes. However, Glenn Singleton, coauthor of *Courageous Conversations About Race*, reminds us that while loving our children as unique individuals, we must also become accustomed to seeing the racial mosaic of our biracial and multicultural children.

Glenn suggests that by seeing this beautiful racial mosaic in Eva's skin, eyes, and hair, we also witness

> *the wonderful culture that emerges from her blended background . . . her happiness, curiosity, and intelligence. We are hopeful that these characteristics will continue to shine through as the world attempts to understand the many elders and ancestors from a variety of races that contributed to her stunning image!*

> — G. Singleton (personal communication,
> March 24, 2009)

Thank you, Glenn, for reminding me of the purpose of this journey.

Thank you, courageous Reader, for taking this journey with me! Please contact me and tell me about your journey at a4achievement@earthlink.net

Selected Bibliography

American Anthropological Association. (1998). *American Anthropological Association's statement on race.* Retrieved June 24, 2008, from http://www.aaanet.org/issues/policy-advocacy/AAA-Statement-on-Race.cfm

Bolgatz, J. (2005). *Talking race in the classroom.* NY: Teachers College Press.

Burrello, K. N. (n.d.). What are the strengths of interracial families? Retrieved May 11, 2008, from http://www.diversitydtg.com/articles/interracial_families.htm

Childs, E. (2005). *Navigating interracial borders: Black-white couples and their social worlds.* Piscataway, NJ: Rutgers University Press.

DaCosta, K. M. (2007). *Making multiracials: State, family, and market in the redrawing of the color line.* Stanford, CA: Stanford University Press.

Davis, B. (2006). *How to teach students who don't look like you: Culturally relevant teaching strategies.* Thousand Oaks, CA: Corwin.

Delgado, R., & Stefancic, J. (Eds.). (1997). Critical race theory: An annotated bibliography. *Virginia Law Review, 79,* 461–516.

Dutro, E., Kazemi, E., & Balf, R. (2005, November). The aftermath of "you're only half": Multiracial identities in the literacy classroom. *Language Arts, 83*(2), 96–106.

Gaskins, P. (1999). *What are you? Voices of mixed-race young people.* NY: Henry Holt and Company.

Gay, G. (2000). *Culturally responsive teaching: Theory, research, and practice.* NY: Teachers College Press.

Harris, H. L. (2006, Spring/Fall). African American school counselors: Their perceptions of biracial individuals. *Journal of Professional Counseling: Practice, Theory, and Research, 34*(1&2).

Henze, R., Norte, E., Sather, S. E., & Walker, E. (2002). *Leading for diversity: How school leaders promote interethnic relations.* Thousand Oaks, CA: Corwin.

Jones, N. A., & Smith, A. S. (2000). *U.S. Census Bureau: The two or more races population: 2000.* Census 2000 Brief Series C2KBR/0I-6, 2001. http://www.census.gov/prod/2001pubs/c2kbroi-6.pdf.

Landsman, J. (2001). *A white teacher talks about race.* Lanham, Maryland: Scarecrow Press.

Lindsey, R. (2005). *The culturally proficient school: An implementation guide for school leaders.* Thousand Oaks, CA: Corwin.

Myrdal, G. (1996). *An American dilemma: The Negro problem and modern democracy (Black and African American studies)* (Vol. 2). Piscataway, NJ: Transaction Publishers.

Nakazawa, D. J. (2003). The identity development of the 11-to-14-year-old multiracial youth. In M. Root & M. Kelley (Eds.), *Multiracial child resource book: Living complex identities* (p. 71). Seattle, WA: Mavin Foundation.

Obama, B. (1995). *Dreams from my father: A story of race and inheritance.* NY: Three Rivers Press.

O'Hearn, C. (1998). *Half and half: Writers on growing up biracial and bicultural.* NY: Pantheon Books.

Pollock, M. (2008). *Everyday antiracism: Getting real about race in school.* NY: The New Press.

Robins, N. K., Lindsey, R. B., Lindsey, D. B., & Terrell, R. (2002). *Culturally proficient instruction: A guide for people who teach.* Thousand Oaks, CA: Corwin.

Rockquemore, K., & Laszloffy, T. (2005). *Raising biracial children.* Lanham, MD: Rowman & Littlefield.

Root, M, (Ed.). (1992). *Racially mixed people in America.* Thousand Oaks, CA: Sage.

Root, M. (2001). *Love's revolution: Interracial marriage.* Philadelphia, PA: Temple University Press.

Root, M., & Kelley, M. (Eds.). (2003). *Multiracial child resource book: Living complex identities.* Seattle, WA: Mavin Foundation.

Schreck, M. K. (2009). *Transformers: Creative teachers for the 21st century.* Thousand Oaks, CA: Corwin.

Singleton, G., & Linton, C. (2006). *Courageous conversations about race: A field guide for achieving equity in schools.* Thousand Oaks, CA: Corwin.

Spencer, R. (2006). *Challenging multiracial identity.* Boulder, CO: Lynne Rienner Publishers.

Spickard, P. (1989). *Mixed blood: Intermarriage and ethnic identity in twentieth-century America.* Madison, WI: The University of Wisconsin Press.

Squires, C. R. (2007). *Dispatches from the color line: The press and multiracial America.* Albany, NY: State University of New York Press.

Terrell, R., & Lindsey, R. (2009). *Culturally proficient leadership: The personal journey begins within.* Thousand Oaks, CA: Corwin.

Wallace, K. (2001). Incorporating multiracial/multiethnic topics in teacher preparation: Pedagogical and ideological considerations [Electronic version]. *Electronic Magazine of Multicultural Education, 3*(2). Retrieved June 11, 2008, from http://www.easternedu/publications/emme/2001fall/wallace.html.

Wardle, F. (1992, May). Supporting biracial children in the school setting. *Education & Treatment of Children, 15*(2).

Wardle, F. (1999/2000, December/January). Children of mixed race—no longer invisible. *Educational Leadership. 57*(4), 68–72. Retrieved June 11, 2008, from http://ascd.org/ed_topics/ell99912_wardle.html.

Williams, L. (2002). *It's the little things: The everyday interactions that anger, annoy, and divide the races.* NY: Harcourt.

Winters, L. I., & DeBose, H. (2003). *New faces in a changing America: Multiracial identity in the 21st century.* Thousand Oaks, CA: Sage.

Wise, T. (2008). *White like me: Reflections on race from a privileged son.* Brooklyn, NY: Soft Scull Press.

Yosso, T. (2006). *Critical race counterstories along the chicana/chicano educational pipeline.* NY: Routledge.

Zack, N. (2002). *Philosophy of science and race.* NY: Routledge.

Index

CORWIN

A SAGE Company

The Corwin logo—a raven striding across an open book—represents the union of courage and learning. Corwin is committed to improving education for all learners by publishing books and other professional development resources for those serving the field of PreK–12 education. By providing practical, hands-on materials, Corwin continues to carry out the promise of its motto: **"Helping Educators Do Their Work Better."**